DISBELIEVING
DISBELIEF

How the New Atheists make atheism unbelievable

EDITED BY
PHILLIP BROWN

CHALLENGE BOOKS

Challenge Books
508 High St
Preston Vic. 3072
Australia

Challenge Books is an imprint of Mosaic Resources Pty Ltd

ISBN 9781743241394

Compilation copyright © Phillip Brown 2012
The copyright of individual chapters remains with the authors.

First published 2012

Cataloguing-in-Publication entry is available for the National Library of
Australia http:/catalogue.nla.gov.au/.

Typesetting design by Jock Allan
Cover design by John Healy
Printed and bound in Great Britain by
Marston Book Services Limited, Oxfordshire

Contents

Dedicated to

Stephen K. Brown, my first teacher on solid Christian thinking

Acknowledgments

There have been many people involved in helping get this book together. First and foremost, I would like to thank the authors for their valued contribution to understanding the New Atheism movement. I would also like to acknowledge that many authors come from families that allowed their fathers and husbands the time to think and write on this subject and for that I am forever grateful. Due thanks needs to be given to Jocelyn Penington and Julie Umek for their editing work. I am also grateful to Peter Adam for his prayers and counsel as well as writing the foreword to the book. Thanks also to the congregation of St John's Anglican Church West Brunswick, Melbourne, where many conversations on atheism and apologetics take place.

Foreword

Peter Adam

Former Principal of Ridley Melbourne and Vicar Emeritus of St Jude's Anglican Church Carlton

Disbelieving Disbelief.

What a splendid title for a book!

We must be reflective sceptics! To be a sane human being currently requires sustained, discerning, wise, strenuous and intentional scepticism, lest we be manipulated by advertisements, by the media, by our sub-culture, by our multi-valued society, by the internet, or by the deep, unarticulated and untested assumptions of the twenty-first century. To sustain Christian identity requires similarly energetic scepticism about ideas and assumptions that are common in our world. We need wisdom to cope with multiple ideas and world-views. We need to learn to recognise, articulate and critique the deepest assumptions that surround us and influence us.

What an important topic!

I meet the ideas of the New Atheism everyday. It is pervasive and powerful in Australia, and I am glad that it is being so clearly articulated by its current international leaders, for the leaders are only expressing what many people feel is the case. The articulation of this world-view by its current leaders serves us well in being able to understand it, and to form our own responses and insights. The idea that the New Atheism has demolished Christianity is a development of the idea that science has demolished Christianity, and will soon be as powerful, pervasive, and persuasive.

What a useful book!

This richly diverse book is a great resource to help us understand the New Atheist claims and how we might respond. In it we travel between the acclaimed leaders of the New Atheism and Aquinas, between science and scientism, between Genesis and the Gospels, between Nick Cave and Dietrich Bonhoeffer, between a critique of the New Atheism and helpful reflections on human life today, and between the articulation of the deep assumptions and methodology of current secularism and a nuanced analysis of Christian believing. The authors bring a variety of backgrounds and interests to provide stimulating ways of tackling the topic. And how appropriate to produce this book in Melbourne, which appears to have added to its identity the role of being a centre for New Atheist pilgrimage!

This is a timely, useful, and stimulating book, and I thank the editor and authors for their helpful work.

Introduction: Bringing Down the Religious Twin Towers

Phillip Brown

On September 2001 the world changed forever,[1] four commercial jet aircrafts were hijacked and used as weapons against targets on the soil of the United States of America. Two were deliberately flown into the Twin Towers of the World Trade Center in New York City and another single aircraft into the Pentagon. The fourth never made in to its target in Washington D.C. with the passengers forcing the aircraft down into a field many miles before its designated goal.

Nearly 3000 innocent victims lost their lives that day and the Western world suddenly realised a terrorist threat in a manner never seen before. The aftermath of such a horrendous event has been felt right through airports in the United States and around the globe. The terrorist attack left its impact not just in the buildings, planes and lives destroyed but it even sent its tentacles outwards, to influence construction on future skyscraper buildings and global politics amongst others. Who was to blame? In 2004 Al-Qaeda's leader, Osama bin Laden, appeared on Arabic television and claimed responsibility.[2] The United States of America responded by invading Afghanistan and declaring war on Terror. In 2011 Osama bin Laden was found, captured and killed in Pakistan. What could have motivated a man to orchestrate such mass murder and what's more to actually achieve it? Was it the east versus Western capitalism? Was it revenge attacks on past American interference? Was it the Islamic faith issuing jihad, the holy war against unbelievers in the United States? Or was it religion in general?

Almost a year after Osama bin Laden admitted responsibility to the 9/11 attacks in America, author Sam Harris wrote and had published a book arguing that it was religious belief that fuelled such an atrocious event. This claim by Harris was made in spite of evidence that the hijackers were part of an organisation with political objectives, which were to force American troops out of Saudi Arabia, to undermine its traditional support for Israel and to stop its bombing of Iraq.[3] His book, *The end Of faith* disputed the benefits of religious belief against pure reason, which leads ineffably to mankind's willingness to suspend reason in support of religious beliefs, even when these beliefs instigate the worst of human carnage. Harris' diagnosis of the root problem in the 9/11 attacks certainly appeared to resonate with many people, with his book becoming a New York Times best seller. Furthermore, he sparked more like-minded arguments against religion and in 2006 Oxford biologist and public evolutionist, Richard Dawkins published *The God Delusion,* also topping the best sellers list. These books were shortly followed a year later by two more best sellers, one written by a philosopher, Daniel Dennett titled *Breaking The Spell,* and the other by an author and columnists Christopher Hitchens, titled *God is not great.* These four authors have now become known as the 'four horsemen' of the anti-apocalypse, in a mocking of the imagery of the four horseman pictured in the last book of the Bible. They are also the co-founders of the anti religious movement The 'New Atheists'.

What is so new about this 'New Atheism', when clearly there have been atheists in the past who have written books and made similar statements? Of course, but there is one massive difference, a difference that is breeding intolerance and hatred of anything even faintly smelling religious. Harris, Dawkins, Hitchens and Dennett's brand of atheism is different in that they see it as the antidote to the cultural poison that religion is on our world.

The four horsemen of the anti-apocalypse have not only sold millions of copies of their anti-religious books but they have birthed a whole brand of 'New Atheist' authors who have taken up the gauntlet laid down by Dawkins and others.

Are they correct in their assessment? They may well be, and if so then careful and focused attention should be paid to what they are saying. This is what I initially started to do by buying and reading these books when they were published. I was at that time a student of theology at Ridley Melbourne, studying to become an ordained minister in the Anglican Church. What I found whilst reading them, however, was not a careful analysis of religion and its destructive impacts on humanity but rather an angry, misinformed, prejudicial and a blatantly intolerant attack on religion in all forms. In an ironic twist it appeared to me that the 'New Atheists' had hijacked ill-informed impressions and assumptions about the world's religions and were using them to blindly fly into organised religion with the hope that this initial explosion would cause the 'religious towers' to metaphorically fall and fatally cripple religion forever.

This collection of essays makes an effort to expose exactly what and how the New Atheists are saying about religion. These subjects written on range from science to philosophy, logic to popular culture and all deal directly with what the New Atheist see as problems with active religious faith in Australia. All the authors have particular interests in the New Atheism movement.

---

[1] The introduction was read by the author as part of a motion to engage with *The Global Atheist Convention –A Celebration of Reason*, for the Melbourne Anglican Diocese 2011 Synod.
[2] Robertson, Geoffrey. *Crimes Against Humanity*. (London: Penguin, 2008), 517
[3] Ibid. 517.

Chapter 1: The New Atheism

An introduction and overview

Robert Martin

The New Atheism: an overview: 'the four horsemen'

The New Atheism is a modern, popular and militant form of atheism. It is its militancy which distinguishes it as 'new' and the unifying concept of the New Atheists is 'that we have all decided that the traditional atheist policy of diplomatic reticence [towards religion] should be discarded'.[1] The New Atheists share a belief that religion should not simply be tolerated but should be countered, criticised and exposed by rational argument wherever its influence arises.[2]

The main protagonists of this antireligious apocalypse are the 'four horsemen': Richard Dawkins, Sam Harris, Daniel Dennett, and the late Christopher Hitchens.[3] They all have websites, Facebook pages, and have published bestsellers with huge sales.[4] There are other New Atheist writers including Michel Onfray, Victor Stenger, A. C. Grayling and Robert Park.[5] However, it is primarily the four horsemen who have captured public attention and are visibly identified as the leaders of this movement.

The New Atheism: on religion

The New Atheists see all religion in three ways: irrational, immoral, and obstructionist. I will outline each in turn.

Religion is irrational: The New Atheists crave rationality and empirical evidence.[6] Dawkins writes, 'Have you ever wondered how we know the things we know?'[7] ... The answer ... is "evidence". To the New Atheists science provides this rationality and empirical evidence. They view science as rational and epistemologically superior: '[T]here is no better source of truth on any topic than well-conducted science'.[8] '"Science" represents our best efforts to know what is true in the world'.[9] Indeed the core of science is elevated to the position of 'intellectual honesty'.[10]

This is fundamentally contrasted with religion, which they see as not based on evidence, but on faith. And to the New Atheism the very definition of faith is belief in the absence of evidence. Harris defines faith as 'unjustified belief'.[11] According to Dawkins faith is 'blind trust, in the absence of evidence, even in the teeth of evidence',[12] a definition he continues to uphold, 'Faith is an evil precisely because it requires no justification and brooks no argument'.[13] Grayling goes even further, claiming that faith is a 'commitment to belief contrary to evidence *and* reason'.[14] Moreover, not only do religions require faith, there is no evidence for religious propositions: 'Every religion preaches the truth of propositions for which it has no evidence'.[15] Behind all religion 'there is nothing but bluff,'[16] religious beliefs are 'superdumb'.[17] All religious instincts, beliefs and practices can all be explained naturally[18] and what is not presently explained *will* be explained by science.[19] With science occupying epistemic supremacy, the New Atheists see it opposed to religion and religion opposed to science—they cannot be reconciled.

In summary, the New Atheists believe the findings of science to be evidence-based, whereas religion has no basis in evidence and is essentially irrational. Science is rational and justified; religion is unjustified and based on faith.

Religion is immoral (and dangerous): The New Atheists propose that religion doesn't lead people to live any more morally than the non-religious. In fact, *religion invariably leads to divisions and violence.* Therefore religion is dangerous: religion is 'the most potent source of human conflict, past and present'.[20] Religion motivates otherwise sane people to appalling acts of violence: Dawkins cites the example of Paul Hill, a Christian who murdered an abortion doctor. Dawkins describes him as 'dangerously religious'.[21] Dennett quotes Steven Weinberg: 'Good people will do good things, and bad people will do bad things ... but for good people to do bad things—that takes religion'.[22] The 9/11 terrorist attacks on the World Trade Center are held up as the prime example,[23] and have proved to be an important catalyst for the New Atheist movement. Indeed Sam Harris claims to have begun writing *The End of Faith* on September 12, 2001.[24] Furthermore, the appalling morality of the Bible and the bloodthirsty character of God give us nothing worthwhile to imitate, it is suggested. The authors outline with relish the perceived barbarity of the Bible, particularly the Old Testament. Hitchens described the Old Testament as a 'nightmare' full of pitiless genocide, stonings, slavery and witch hunts,[25] with God as 'dictator'.[26] Dawkins concurs, and describes the God of the Old Testament as 'arguably the most unpleasant character in all fiction'.[27] Dennett suggests that we would not be comfortable living under the ethical prohibitions and requirements of the Old Testament.[28] The New Testament also receives condemnation as morally abhorrent. Jesus endorsed the 'barbarity' of the Old Testament Law,[29] possessed 'dodgy family values'[30] and encouraged 'out-group hostility'.[31] Dawkins in particular is caustic towards the doctrine of atonement, describing it as 'vicious, sado-masochistic and repellent'.[32] In summary, according to the New Atheism movement, religion doesn't deliver moral improvement or model proper moral behaviour. Instead religion is dangerous and 'positively immoral'.[33]

Religion is obstructionist: As outlined earlier the New Atheists see religion and science as fundamentally opposed and any attempt to reconcile the two is dishonest. Therefore, *religion obstructs scientific research.* The wonders of the microbial world were only made evident after, 'the priests had been elbowed aside and medical research at last given an opportunity'.[34] Stem-cell research, 'one of the most promising developments in the last century of medicine' is hindered by religious interference.[35] Furthermore, Hitchens claimed that religion used to *prevent* the emergence of rivals, whereas now it can 'only impede and retard—or try to turn back—the measurable [scientific] advances that we have made'.[36] Furthermore they suggest that invoking God as a solution to scientific difficulties (a God of the gaps) is willful ignorance and is opposed to further scientific enquiry as Dawkins enthusiastically points out:

Here is the message that an imaginary 'intelligent design theorist' might broadcast to scientists: 'If you don't understand how something works, never mind: just give up and say God did it ... Dear scientists, don't *work* on your mysteries. Bring us your mysteries, for we can use them. Don't squander precious ignorance by researching it away. We need those glorious gaps as a last refuge for God'.[37]

Moreover, religion *obstructs otherwise 'rational' ethical decision-making*. For example, Dawkins suggests that many of the ethical difficulties surrounding abortion evaporate when a 'non-religious consequentialist moral philosophy' is adopted at the expense of 'religiously absolute moral philosophies'.[38] Religion also *obstructs otherwise pleasurable pastimes (usually surrounding sex)*. For example, drug use, homosexuality,[39] masturbation,[40] or premarital sex.[41] Harris notes the concern people with faith make over such situations: '[Your] principle concern appears to be that the creator of the universe will take offence at something people do while naked'.[42] Furthermore religion perpetuates human suffering by opposing certain 'immoral' actions, such as promoting abstinence rather than condom use.[43] Moreover *religion obstructs otherwise intelligent people from realising their full potential.* Religion ruins the scientific education of many promising young minds.[44] Indoctrinating children to religion is a form of child abuse.[45] Faith chokes free inquiry;[46] and religion keeps the Amish trapped in the seventeenth century.[47] Indeed competing religious certainties impede the emergence of a viable, global civilization.[48] The New Atheism presents religion as oppressive and obstructionist.

The New Atheism conclusions regarding religion

Religion should be actively opposed (and, ideally, eliminated): The New Atheists suggest that there is no 'mild' form of religion. It is irrational, immoral, and obstructionist in any form, and 'even mild and moderate religion helps to provide the climate of faith in which extremism naturally flourishes'.[49] The enemy is not Islam or extremism, the enemy is 'nothing other than faith itself'.[50] Thus the New Atheists, armed with modern scientific rationalism, implore modern society to grow up and finally put an end to religion. As the New Atheists webpage declares: '[We] are smart enough now to kill our invisible gods and oppressive beliefs'.[51] This forms the heart of the New Atheist manifesto. The uniting characteristic of their catechesis is 'that [they] have all decided that the traditional atheist policy of diplomatic reticence should be discarded'.[52] This is the most significant factor defining the 'new' from the 'old' atheism. Interestingly this active, militant opposition has led to confusion over the degree of 'toleration' afforded to religion. Whilst Dennett claims the four horsemen *tolerate* religion,[53] some of their followers have taken this opposition a step further *promoting* the 'intolerance of [and]' 'disregard of tolerance for religion'.[54]

Religion should not participate in the formulation of public policy: New Atheist confusion over the level of toleration afforded to religion spills into the arena of public policy. Despite Dennett's protestations of New Atheist toleration, Harris and Hitchens adopt a fundamentally *intolerant* position with respect to religion's role in the public amphitheatre. Sam Harris claims the primary purpose for writing *Letter to a Christian Nation* was 'to arm secularists in our society, who believe that religion should be kept out of public policy'.[55] Hitchens also called for religion to be banished from ethical public discourse accordingly.[56]

The world would be a better place without religion: The new atheists confidently assert that atheism offers freedom from all of the problems religion brings. With religion out of the way, an atheistic society would offer rational freedom and opportunity for unconstrained, unfettered research, thought and behaviour. This explains the urgency of their undertaking to promote their world-view, the '[indoctrination] of logic, reason and the advancement of a naturalistic worldview'.[57] The New Atheists concede that atheists can do bad things. However, atheism is not the driving force, since '[individual] atheists may do evil things but they don't do evil things in the name of atheism'.[58] They claim that atheism rarely causes people to do immoral things. In fact, Harris claims the atheist tyrants were not rational[59] and Dawkins suggests the evil Stalin and Hitler committed was not done in the name of atheism but in the name of 'dogmatic and doctrinaire Marxism, and an insane and unscientific eugenics theory tinged with sub-Wagnerian ravings'.[60]

According to Hitchens, totalitarian societies were in fact theocracies, intimately bound with religion.[61] He also claimed the brutal, atheistic, totalitarian, communist leaders were simply seeking to 'replace' religion, not negate it,[62] implying that they weren't *really* atheistic states, just another form of fundamentalist religious totalitarianism. The New Atheists conclude that atheism is not only intellectually more rational, but morally more acceptable. The New Atheists consistently propose that the end of religion should be celebrated, not mourned. They crave a 'renewed Enlightenment'.[63]

Further observations on the New Atheism

The New Atheism is a popular modern social phenomenon, but there are a number of other observations to be made about the New Atheists and their work. The first is that they are all wonderful rhetoricians. The four horsemen are gifted writers and communicators.[64] While this has undoubtedly contributed to their public appeal and influence, they are, in general confrontational name-callers demonstrating little respect for opponents.[65] For example, Hitchens derided the intelligent design 'boobies'.[66] Augustine was as a 'self-centred fantasist and an earth-centred ignoramus'.[67] As an argument for God's existence the ontological argument is, 'infantile'.[68] Furthermore, the Bible and Koran both contain 'mountains of life-destroying gibberish'[69] and the God of the Old Testament is a 'petty, unjust, unforgiving, control-freak; a vindictive, bloodthirsty ethnic cleanser; a misogynistic, homophobic, racist, infanticidal, genocidal, filicidal, pestilential, megalomaniacal, sadomasochistic, capriciously malevolent bully'.[70] This confrontational element is a notable constituent part of the New Atheism and stems from their militant position. With reason and the 'salvation' that evolutionary theory offers,[71] the New Atheists seek to 'demolish the intellectual and moral pretensions'[72] of the enemy, be the enemy 'Christianity'[73], 'faith'[74] or 'religion' more generally.[75]

There are several reasons for their militancy. It partly stems from the perceived urgency of their task. The 9/11 terrorist attacks are used as consistent proof of the danger religion poses; hence the world urgently needs to stop religion before it can do more damage. Second, their militancy rests on *a commitment to rationality and a sure belief that they are right:* '[Nothing] is more sacred than the facts'.[76] And they believe that through their epistemology (scientific empiricism) they correctly interpret the facts.[77] Third, their epistemology fails to allow them ambiguity in debate, and as such they present complex issues in a simplistic manner. The New Atheists see the world in black and white, often from a scientific perspective, and fail to appreciate subtlety in debate. For example, Harris makes a simplistic presentation of the 'problem of evil' and 'solves' it![78] Stenger's presentation of 'logical disproofs for the existence of God' is another example, claiming that these are inescapable unless you 'change the rules of the game or, more commonly, change the definitions of the words being used in the argument'.[79] Hitchens asserted that 'all attempts to reconcile faith with science and reason are consigned to failure and ridicule'.[80] Allied to this and more disturbingly, the New Atheists consistently fail to present alternative views fairly. Rarely do the New Atheists enter into a robust discussion of the issues engaging key contributors.[81] Discussions are distorted, contorted, shortened and vastly simplified.[82] They consistently portray their opponents via straw-men. Dawkins's definition of faith 'as blind trust' is recognised as such by McGrath.[83] Dawkins's discussion on the 'argument from scripture' as evidence for belief in God, arguably the strongest theistic argument used by many, is treated in only six pages.[84] The 'argument from admired religious scientists'—an argument rarely, if ever, used by any apologist—receives more space![85] In attempting to demonstrate the 'corrupt beginnings' of religion Hitchens didn't look at the early textual history of the New Testament. Instead he examined the Melanesian cargo cults, the Pentecostal superstar Marjoe and the Mormons![86] Dawkins summarises the way in which scripture might be a source of morals or rules for living in only two ways: 'divine command' and 'imitation'.[87] There is no reference to major thinkers to support his assertion, and no discussion of the various ways Christian ethicists have approached the issue.[88] This simple, clear-cut approach, arguing from extremes as if normative, may make the New Atheists popular, but it weakens their intellectual credibility. Unfortunately their credibility is further weakened by some of their number (notably Hitchens and

Dawkins)[89] being guilty of sloppy scholarship. Fairly basic errors riddle their work. Dawkins discusses the 'worship by kings' in Luke's infancy narrative (they occur in Matthew 2:1-12),[90] he confuses the Gospel of Thomas with the Infancy Gospel of Thomas,[91] and quotes Tertullian as saying 'It is by all means to be believed, because it is absurd',[92] though he said no such thing.[93] Hitchens got several (recent) dates wrong, suggesting the devastating Asian Tsunami occurred in 2005, (it was December 2004),[94] and New Orleans was inundated in 2006 (it was August 2005).[95] He also suggests that all four Gospels 'may possibly have been based' on the 'speculative' book of Q (it is commonly proposed as a hypothetical source for the sayings of Jesus found in Matthew and Luke and not Mark).[96] Occasional scholarly lapses are easily forgiven. However, these consistent, basic errors of scholarship are disturbing from a group claiming intellectual superiority. Finally, it is likely that part of the militancy of the New Atheism comes as a response to the militancy of their chief opponents—fundamentalists, particularly American Protestant fundamentalists,[97] and Islamic extremism.[98] The irony is that by virtue of its total dogmatic conviction of correctness, misrepresentation of its opponents, and simplistic reasoning, the New Atheism itself becomes aligned with a form of militant religious fundamentalism, 'which refuses to allow its ideas to be examined or challenged'.[99]

---

[1] Daniel Dennett commenting on Andrew Brown's blog, *The Guardian* (accessed July 13, 2009),
http://www.guardian.co.uk/commentisfree/andrewbrown/2008/dec/29/religion-new-atheism-defined?showallcomments=true

[2] Simon Hooper, 'The Rise of the "New Atheists"', *CNN* (accessed July 7, 2009),
http://www.cnn.com/2006/WORLD/europe/11/08/atheism.feature/index.html

[3] The 'four horsemen' originally described Richard Dawkins, Sam Harris, Daniel Dennett, and Carl Sagan. David P. Barash, 'The DNA of Religious Faith', *The Chronicle of Higher Education,* 53/33 (20 April 2007): B6, http://chronicle.com/weekly/v53/i33/33b00601.htm. (accessed July 7, 2009). Reprinted in full at http://www.samharris.org/site/full_text/the-dna-of-religious-faith/. However, Sagan died in 1986 and Christopher Hitchens has taken his place. See 'The Four Horsemen: A Round Table Discussion With Richard

Dawkins, Daniel C. Dennett, Sam Harris, Christopher Hitchens,' *Discussions with Richard Dawkins*, no. 1 (2007).

[4] Richard Dawkins, *The God Delusion* (more than 2 million sales). As at mid-2007: Christopher Hitchens' *God Is Not Great* (296,000 sales); Sam Harris', *Letter to a Christian Nation*, (185,000 sales); *The End of Faith*, (over 400,000 sales) and Daniel Dennett's *Breaking the Spell*, (64,000 sales). Print figures from David Aikman, *The Delusion of Disbelief: Why the New Atheism Is a Threat to Your Life, Liberty, and Pursuit of Happiness*, (Carol Stream: Tyndale, 2008), 1-2. More data at: http://www.publishersweekly.com/article/CA6448568.html.

[5] Michel Onfray, *The Atheist Manifesto: The Case Against Christianity, Judaism and Islam*, (Melbourne: Melbourne University Press, 2005); Victor Stenger, *God: The Failed Hypothesis: How Science Shows That God Does Not Exist*, (Amherst: Prometheus Books, 2007); A. C. Grayling, *Against All Gods: Six Polemics on Religion and an Essay on Kindness*, (London: Oberon, 2007); Grayling, 'Believers Are Away With The Fairies', *The Telegraph* (accessed September 11, 2009), http://www.telegraph.co.uk/news/features/3631819/Believers-are-away-with-the-fairies.html Cited: 11 September 2009; Robert L. Park, *Superstition: Belief in the Age of Science*, (Princeton: Princeton University Press, 2008).

[6] Daniel C Dennett, *Breaking the Spell*, (London: Penguin Books, 2006), 16.

[7] Richard Dawkins, 'Good and Bad Reasons for Believing', in *A Devil's Chaplain: Selected Essays by Richard Dawkins*, ed. Latha Menon, (London: Weidenfield & Nicholson, 2003), 242.

[8] Dennett, *Breaking the Spell*, 372.

[9] Harris, *Letter to a Christian Nation*, (New York: Knopf. 2006), 64.

[10] Harris, *Letter to a Christian Nation*, 64.

[11] Harris, *The End of Faith*, (New York: W. W. Norton, 2004), 65.

[12] Richard Dawkins, *The Selfish Gene*, (London: Paladin/Granada, 1978), 212.

[13] Dawkins, *The God Delusion*, (London: Bantam Books, 2006), 308. This is despite it being shown as inadequate by Alister McGrath (Alister McGrath, *Dawkins' God: Genes, Memes, and the Meaning of Life*, (Oxford: Blackwell, 2005), 84-91.)

[14] Grayling, *Against All Gods*, (London: Oberon Books, 2007), 15. Italics mine.

[15] Harris, *The End of Faith*, 23.

[16] Hitchens, *God Is Not Great*, (New York: Twelve Books, 2007), 150.

[17] Richard Dawkins, 'Atheists for Jesus?', *Free Inquiry*, no.25 vol. 1, 2006: 11.

[18] See: Dennett, *Breaking the Spell*, 97-199; Dawkins, *The God Delusion*, 161-207.

[19] Hitchens, *God Is Not Great*, 86.

[20] Harris, *The End of Faith*, 35.

[21] Dawkins, *The God Delusion*, 296.

[22] Dennett, *Breaking the Spell*, 279.

[23] See for example: Hitchens, *God Is Not Great*, 28-32; Dennett, *Breaking the Spell*, 280-281; Dawkins, *The God Delusion*, 1; Dawkins, 'Atheists for Jesus?', 11; Harris, *The End of Faith*, 29-36.

[24] Harris, *The End of Faith*, 323.

[25] Hitchens, *God Is Not Great*, 97-107.

[26] Hitchens, *God Is Not Great*, 175.

[27] Dawkins, *The God Delusion*, 31.

[28] Dennett in Dennett and McGrath, 'The Future of Atheism: A Dialogue' in *The Future of Atheism: Alister McGrath & Daniel Dennett in Dialogue,* (Minneapolis: Fortress, 2008), 43.

[29] Harris, *Letter to a Christian Nation*, 10.

[30] Dawkins, *The God Delusion*, 251.

[31] Ibid., 254.

[32] Ibid., 253.

[33] Hitchens, *God Is Not Great*, 205.

[34] Ibid., 90.

[35] Harris, *Letter to a Christian Nation*, 28-29.; see also, Harris, *End of Faith*, 165-167.; Dawkins, *The God Delusion*, 294.

[36] Hitchens, *God Is Not Great*, 282. Italics original.

[37] Dawkins, *The God Delusion*, 132, see also 284-86.

[38] Ibid., 291-298, part. 297.

[39] Harris, *The End of Faith*, 160.; Dawkins, *The God Delusion*, 289-291.

[40] Hitchens, *God Is Not Great*, 226-227.

[41] Harris, *Letter to a Christian Nation*, 26.

[42] Ibid.

[43] Harris, *The End of Faith*, 167-69.

[44] Dawkins, *The God Delusion*, 284-286.

[45] Dawkins, *The God Delusion*, 311-340.; Hitchens, *God Is Not Great*, 217-228.

[46] Hitchens, *God Is Not Great*, 137.

---

[47] Dawkins, *The God Delusion*, 331.

[48] Harris, *Letter to a Christian Nation*, 80.

[49] Dawkins, *The God Delusion*, 303.

[50] Harris, *The End of Faith*, 131.

[51] The New Atheists, 'The New Atheists', (accessed July 7, 2009). http://newatheists.org/

[52] Andrew Brown blog, (accessed July 7, 2009) http://www.guardian.co.uk/commentisfree/andrewbrown/2008/dec/29/religion-new-atheism-defined?showallcomments=true

[53] Dennett, personal email.

[54] The New Atheism, 'The New Atheism' (accessed July 13, 2009) http://newatheism.org/. This webpage (and www.newatheists.org) is not officially endorsed by the four horsemen, (Dennett, personal email), though it contains links to them all.

[55] Harris, *Letter to a Christian Nation*, viii.

[56] Hitchens, *God Is Not Great*, 283.

[57] The New Atheism, 'The New Atheism', (accessed July 13, 2009), http://newatheism.org/

[58] Dawkins, *The God Delusion*, 278.

[59] Harris, *Letter to a Christian Nation*, 42.

[60] Dawkins, *The God Delusion*, 278.

[61] Hitchens, *God Is Not Great*, 232.

[62] Ibid., 246.

[63] Ibid., 283.

[64] A view shared by David Marshall, *The Truth Behind the New Atheism*, (Eugene: Harvest House, 2007), 12.

[65] Daniel Dennett is the notable exception. However it must also be noted Dennett's books have not sold nearly as well. This may indicate that much of the new atheism is personality driven sensationalism.

[66] Hitchens, *God Is Not Great*, 269.

[67] Ibid., 64.

[68] Dawkins, *The God Delusion*, 80.

[69] Harris, *The End of Faith*, 23.

[70] Dawkins, *The God Delusion*, 31.

[71] Dennett, *Breaking the Spell*, 268.

[72] Harris, *Letter to a Christian Nation*, ix.

[73] Ibid.

[74] Harris, *The End of Faith*, 131.

[75] Hitchens, *God Is Not Great*, 283.

[76] Harris, *The End of Faith*, 225.

[77] Ironically only one of the four horsemen is actually a scientist! Dawkins is the only true scientist amongst the troupe. Dennett and Harris are quasi-scientists; Dennett is a philosopher by training but claims to work 'in and on the edges of science and evolutionary biology, evolutionary theory, cognitive science and psychology', Daniel Dennett in Dennett and McGrath, 'The Future of Atheism: A Dialogue', in *The Future of Atheism: Alister McGrath & Daniel Dennett in Dialogue*, (Minneapolis: Fortress, 2008), 20. Harris has a degree in philosophy and a doctorate in neuro-science. Hitchens had no scientific credentials and was a journalist.

[78] Harris, *Letter to a Christian Nation*, 55.

[79] Stenger, *God: The Failed Hypothesis*, 31.

[80] Hitchens, *God Is Not Great*, 64-65.

[81] Dennett is generally better in this regard, but not entirely exonerated. For example, he fails to discuss important counter evidence at any length. In his (all too brief discussion) section 'Does God exist?' he dismisses the validity of the inclusion of the Gospels in the discussion as 'manifestly question begging'. He buttresses this assertion with reference to the *Book of Mormon* and L. Ron Hubbard's *Dianetics,* (New York: Hermitage House, 1950). He ignores the historical claims of the New Testament and moves onto philosophical arguments for the existence of God, which he appears to be more comfortable and capable of discussing (see: Dennett, *Breaking the Spell*, 240-241).

[82] A point also noted by Tina Beattie, *The New Atheists: The Twilight of Reason & the War on Religion,* (London: Darton, Longman & Todd, 2007), 121.

[83] McGrath, *Dawkins' God*, 86.

[84] Dawkins, *The God Delusion*, 92-97

[85] Ibid., 97-103.

[86] Hitchens, *God Is Not Great*, 155-168.

[87] Dawkins, *The God Delusion*, 237.

[88] Christians have approached the role of the Bible in ethics in many more sophisticated ways than Dawkins presents.

[89] Onfray is also guilty of basic scholarly errors, claiming Augustine wrote a letter in 185, some 170 years before his birth (Onfray, *The Atheist Manifesto,* 190.); he quotes 2 Cor 2:210 (Onfray, *The Atheist Manifesto,* 134); he also accuses the Gospels of historical inaccuracy by referring to Pilate as procurator instead of prefect—yet the Gospels make no such claim. (Onfray, *The Atheist Manifesto,* 128).

[90] Dawkins, *The God Delusion,* 94.

[91] Ibid., 96. Pointed out by Marshall, *The Truth Behind the New Atheism,* 121.

[92] Richard Dawkins, 'Viruses of the Mind' in *A Devil's Chaplain: Selected Essays by Richard Dawkins,* 139.

[93] Pointed out by McGrath, *Dawkins' God,* 100.

[94] Hitchens, *God Is Not Great,* 148.

[95] Ibid., 149.

[96] Ibid., 112. Admittedly Q can refer to the cycle of oral tradition circulating in the early church but this was not written as Hitchens suggests. For more detail see, G.N. Stanton, 'Q' in *Dictionary of Jesus and the Gospels,* ed. Joel B. Green and Scot McKnight (Downers Grove: Intervarsity Press, 1992), 644.

[97] Noted by Alister McGrath about Dennett's *Breaking the Spell* [Alister McGrath in Dennett and McGrath, 'The Future of Atheism: A Dialogue', in *The Future of Atheism: Alister McGrath & Daniel Dennett in Dialogue,* (Minneapolis: Fortress, 2008), 29].

[98] Beattie, *The New Atheists,* 5.

[99] Alister McGrath and Joanna Collicutt McGrath, *The Dawkins Delusion?: Atheist Fundamentalism and the Denial of the Divine,* (Downers Grove: Intervarsity Press, 2007), xii.

Chapter 2: Speaking Across The Void

World-views, presuppositions and why we must

Simon Angus

[Scene: A cafe on a major university campus. Two scientists share a coffee.]

John: Did you see the article on the news last night, about the guy whose cancer was cured in a day?

Richard: Oh yes, wonderful, wasn't it!

John: Indeed. And such a bad prognosis—he was given only a month to live. Can you imagine it?

Richard: No, I can't. Cancer is... frightening.

[pause]

John: Did you see he had Christian friends who prayed for him for months?

Richard: *[a smile breaks across his face]* Here you go again! I bet you think that your crazy 'God' cured him. *[makes elaborate gestures with his hands]* The "Flying Spaghetti Monster" comes to the rescue again![1]

John: *[smiles]* Well, I guess anyone who's cured is cured by God, ultimately. But this one looks miraculous to me. I wonder if...

Richard: John, John, John ... you and your spiritual mumbo-jumbo! ... 'Miracles' are just your word for unusual events. We've been over this ...

John: But you'd have to admit that it is quite a coincidence: terminal illness, one month to live, prayer by friends, miraculous cure, baffled medicos. What more do you want?[2]

Richard: *[laughs]* But every new cure in the textbook was unusual once, John. You know that. I bet we'll see a hundred people cured of a cancer like this in our lifetime and the medicos will figure out how they did it. Why do you have such a low view of science and medicine?

John: I don't have a low view of science! I just don't think it explains everything we see or experience. In fact, it wasn't ever meant to.

Richard: *[smiles]* Well, between your 'Spaghetti Monster' book and *The Lancet*, I know which one I'll want my specialist to read when I go under the knife!! Let me pay.

[Richard heads to the register. John looks disappointedly after him, before rising to join him.]

***

The Heart of the Matter

What is happening here? What's the nature of the disagreement?

To be sure, John and Richard's disagreement is not over the basic facts of the case: that the man had a serious illness, that he had friends of faith, that they were engaged in prayer for the man's health and, crucially, that the man was healed in an uncommonly short period of time, baffling the expert medical team at his hospital. These are not in doubt.

Instead, their disagreement was over *what agency* had generated those facts.

On the one hand, John was arguing that in all likelihood God had healed the man in a miraculous manner, mercifully responding to the petitions of his faithful friends. On the other hand, Richard saw in these facts no such thing: he saw an entirely mechanistic, though uncommon, immune response to the illness; a case to be celebrated and documented in the annals of science. Indeed, for him, the so-called 'prayer' of his friends was a warm yet ineffectual gesture, unconnected to the recovery.

But the disagreement goes deeper than that, to the very nature of John and Richard's *conception of reality*.

Confronted with the same set of facts, John and Richard were able to fit them precisely in to their own 'world-view'—their own way of interpreting reality. Indeed, as part of this interpretation, both protagonists emphasised or de-emphasised facts along the way. John's *theism* caused him to focus on the link between the prayer and the healing, to emphasise the supernatural dimension to the case (implicitly de-emphasising the role of the medical staff, or the man's own immune system) whilst Richard's *scientism* (a form of atheism) dismissed the role of the prayerful friends, the possibility of miracles (or any spiritual dimension for that matter) instead seeing the man's immune response and expert medical help as the cause of the cure. For Richard, though the specialists didn't perhaps understand how the treatment had worked so well in this case, the scientific method of inquiry would one day reveal it to them.

At heart, John and Richard's disagreement is about the very fundamental nature of the universe. Importantly, these differing prior commitments do not just affect how each *assimilates* facts into their reasoning, but *which facts* are worthy of assimilation and which can be discarded. To borrow a phrase, John and Richard inhabit different 'ideological universes'[3]. Though they might converse on the same physical planet, their minds (and hearts) are like ships passing in the night.

The depressing corollary of this insight is that John and Richard—and countless others across this city—will quite possibly go on having disagreements like the one above every week for the rest of their working lives, speaking the same language, discussing the same topic, but fundamentally failing to connect.

This realisation drives us to wonder: is meaningful dialogue possible? In what follows, I am going to provide some reasons to be optimistic.

To get there, we first need to acquaint ourselves with 'world-view' thinking, and remind ourselves that, consequently, everyone is 'biased' (the Christian being no exception). Second, to help our atheist friends likewise to 'own' this insight, I'll present some evidence on bias, starting with the biblical account and then moving to evidences gleaned from the scientific method. Along the way I will argue that the much-admired position of 'neutrality' is not available to either side in these disagreements, and that the Christian in particular is called to non-neutrality.

My hope is that such considerations will lead to more productive conversations between our 'universes'.

World-views: We've all got them.

What is meant by a 'world-view'?

The term itself is relatively modern, deriving from Immanuel Kant's (1724-1804) passing use of *weltanschauung*, to then be used more intentionally by Wilhelm Dilthey (1833-1911).[4] James Sire has brought world-view thinking to the fore via his popular book, *The Universe Next Door* in which he defines a world-view as,

> A commitment, a fundamental orientation of the heart, that can be expressed as a story or in a set of presuppositions (assumptions which may be true, partially true, or entirely false) which we hold (consciously or subconsciously, consistently or inconsistently) about the basic constitution of reality, and that provides the foundation on which we live and move and have our being.[5]

Some aspects of this definition are worth exploring a little further. Sire uses 'fundamental orientation of the heart' intentionally, since he sees a world-view as all-encompassing and *self*-defining. Our world-view is not simply a set of propositions to which we have given intellectual assent, but shapes our deepest commitments, desires, wishes and character. In short, it is the very stuff of our being. Sire notes that a world-view can be expressed in a variety of ways, 'either as a story, or in a set of presuppositions'. Here, he is being inclusive on mode of expression, allowing either the more postmodern device of 'story-telling' or, alternatively, the propositional language of 'presuppositions' (our 'priors') to express our world-view. Either way, a world-view is something that, 'we [individually] hold' (it is *our* story, *our* set of presuppositions), and it describes our beliefs about, 'the basic constitution of reality'. For Sire, this statement encompasses both an *ontological* as well as an *epistemological* dimensions. That is, a world-view will include our ultimate priors about the force or being upholding reality (ontology), as well as how we might *know* that force or being, or indeed how we arrive at certainty about anything at all (epistemology).

To flesh out the world-view concept and to aid the process of self-discovery of our own or others' world-views, Sire offers the following seven questions that shape a world-view:

1. What is prime reality—the really real?
2. What is the nature of external reality, that is, the world around us?
3. What is a human being?
4. What happens to persons at death?
5. Why is it possible to know anything at all?
6. How do we know what is right and wrong?
7. What is the meaning of human history? [6]

To give an example, the Christian presuppositional apologist John M. Frame offers the following summary of the Christian world-view or presupposition:

> An ultimate presupposition is a basic heart-commitment, an ultimate trust. We trust Jesus Christ as a matter of life or death. We trust his wisdom beyond all other wisdom. We trust his promises above all others. [7]

The myth of 'neutrality'

It is not uncommon in dialogues between atheists and Christians to hear one side or the other suggesting that the dialogue should proceed on purely 'neutral' grounds. That only those facts and methods of reasoning which are mutually agreed upon to be 'non-biased' might be pursued. Behind this suggestion is the prior assumption that an untouched ideological plane exists, one which is common to all other ideological perspectives, and upon which productive dialogue might be enacted. Whilst at first blush such a strategy seems attractive, and indeed has many classical antecedents (e.g. Athenagoras, Theophilus, Aristotides and Thomas Aquinas[8]) world-view (or presuppositional) thinking shows that such a noble pursuit is not in fact possible.

One of the most helpful consequences of world-view thinking is that it brings to the fore a crucial realisation about all of us: world-views are *inescapable*; *we've all got one*. Whether you agree with the importance of the seven questions posed by Sire or not, one cannot leave these questions aside, or ignore their existence. Sire remarks:

> The fact is that we cannot avoid assuming answers to such questions. We will adopt either one stance or another. Refusing to adopt an explicit world-view will turn out to be itself a world-view or at least a philosophic position. In short, we are caught. So long as we live, we will live either the examined or the unexamined life.[9]

Sire's final comment is insightful: the question for each of us is not, ultimately, whether we *have* a world-view, but rather, whether we consciously acknowledge, or 'own' our world-view. Theologian Don Carson reminds us of Carl F. H. Henry's telling observation in the same vein, 'there are two kinds of presuppositionalists: those who admit it and those who don't'.[10] Or, in Sire's language, there are only those who live the 'examined' life on the one hand, or the 'unexamined' life on the other.

As much as 'neutrality' is attractive, world-view thinking shows us that such a country is imaginary. Below, we shall consider the biblical and empirical evidence, which supports this conclusion.

The evidence: Biblical and Empirical

The witness of scripture

Does the God of the Bible see it differently? Does the dichotomy proposed above mesh with the biblical account of life, the universe and everything?

Scripture: Dividing joint and marrow

First, there can be no doubt that scripture proclaims a stark distinction between those who accept the biblical account and those who do not. Or in other words, *non-neutrality* is part and parcel of God's universe. For example, the Apostle Paul writes that 'the word of the cross [of Christ] is folly to those who are perishing, but to us who are being saved it is the power of God'[11]. Or Jesus himself asks, 'Do you think that I have come to give peace on earth? No, I tell you, but rather division'.[12]

The Apostle Paul elaborates on the nature of this division later in his epistle to the Corinthians. After claiming that '[he] decided to know nothing among [the Corinthians] except Jesus Christ and him crucified'[13] the Apostle then teaches that this truth is imparted

> In words not taught by human wisdom but taught by the Spirit, interpreting spiritual truths to those who are spiritual. ... The natural person does not accept the things of the Spirit of God, for they are folly to him, and he is not able to understand them because they are spiritually discerned.[14]

In other words, the claim that Jesus is Lord—the central claim of the Bible—is a kind of truth different to normal wisdom. It is not communicated or apprehended without the help of the Spirit of God, and it will only take root in 'spiritual' people (those who believe and so have the Spirit of God at work in them). Indeed, to the 'natural' person, this word will be 'folly'.

It is important to note that, as opposed to how non-Christian culture thinks of successful communication, the power of Christian communication is not fundamentally drawn from 'lofty speech or wisdom'.[15] Rather, it is the message itself which has the 'power of God'. Biblically, the medium is not the message; the *message* is the message.

Here, the world-view framework is clearly on display. A person's response to the claims of the Bible will immediately demonstrate in which 'camp' a person resides. The claims of God in the Bible will necessarily fashion the fundamental layer of each person's world-view. Indeed, the word of God in scripture is presented as the ultimate world-view defining instrument, described by the writer of Hebrews as 'sharper than any two-edged sword', capable of 'piercing to the division of soul and of spirit, of joints and of marrow, and discerning the thoughts and intentions of the heart'.[16] If ever there were a test of the 'fundamental orientation of the heart', it is here.

Bias of the unbeliever: knowing and suppressing

Second, having divided humanity (and its world-views) by their response to scripture, the Bible presents a humanity that, after The Fall,[17] actively engages in *biased* reasoning against God. The Apostle Paul's argument in the opening chapter of his Epistle to the Romans is damming in this regard. He claims that although all humanity 'knows God' implicitly[18] they have 'become futile in their thinking', their 'foolish hearts' being 'darkened',[19] 'suppress[ing] the truth',[20] and 'exchang[ing] the truth about God for a lie'.[21]

To be clear, the biblical charge is not one of mere *ignorance*. Rather, God's rendition of unregenerate man is that he undeniably 'knows' God, yet he has chosen to suppress that knowledge. An active, intentioned, and deliberate suppression of the truth of the world is his *modus operandi*. This is biased reasoning on the grandest and deepest scale.[22]

Bias of the believer: Jesus Christ is Lord

Finally, lest I leave the impression that scripture teaches that regenerate, or believing, men and women are without bias, let me dispel that suggestion presently. To my mind, scripture conveys nothing so powerfully as it does that the ultimate authority in all matters of truth, knowledge and salvation is uniquely bestowed on the risen Lord Jesus.

Hear the Epistle to the Colossians:

> [Jesus] is the image of the invisible God, the firstborn of all creation. For by him all things were created, in heaven and on earth, visible and invisible, whether thrones or dominions or rulers or authorities—all things were created through him and for him. And he is before all things, and in him all things hold together. And he is the head of the body, the church. He is the beginning, the firstborn from the dead, that in everything he might be pre-eminent.[23]

No comment seems necessary (or adequate). John's famous opening to his account of the life of Jesus is likewise profound:

> In the beginning was the Word [that is, Jesus], and the Word was with God, and the Word was God. He was in the beginning with God. All things were made through Him, and without Him was not any thing made that was made. In Him was life, and the life was the light of men. The light shines in the darkness, and the darkness has not overcome it.[24]

For the one who confesses Christ as Lord, in whom the Spirit has opened their eyes and softened their heart, there is no truth outside of the realm of Christ. As such, there can be no argument made by the believer which does not acknowledge His Lordship.

I finish by recounting the forceful summary on the matter by the Christian apologist John M Frame:

> To tell the unbeliever that [the Christian] can reason with him on a neutral basis, however that claim might help to attract his attention, is a lie. Indeed, it is a lie of the most serious kind, for it falsifies the very heart of the gospel—that Jesus Christ is Lord. For one thing, there is no neutrality. Our witness is either God's wisdom or the world's foolishness. There is nothing in between. For another thing, even if neutrality were possible, that route would be forbidden to us.[25]

The witness of the Sciences

Whilst the previous section will perhaps be a worthwhile witness to the reader who has already accepted Christ, I readily acknowledge that the non-believer will indeed find it 'folly'. As such, let me show where the empirical and social sciences agree with the biblical account, and the bias that world-view thinking introduces in general.

First, psychology, the scientific field most acquainted with the systematic study of human decision-making, has been documenting bias in human reasoning for decades. I will quote from one summary article by R. S. Nickerson published in the *Review of General Psychology*. The article deals primarily with 'confirmation bias', the tendency of humans to filter information, and adapt their reasoning to confirm what they *already believe*. In the article, Nickerson identifies five manifestations of this bias that have been empirically validated.

> 'Restriction of attention to a favoured hypothesis'. Preferential treatment of evidence supporting existing beliefs'.
> 'Looking only or primarily for positive cases'.
> 'Overweighting positive confirmatory instances'.
> 'Seeing what one is looking for'.[26]

(Admittedly, to scientists such as myself, the list is disconcerting.)

Here is precisely the empirical out-workings of the world-view hypothesis. These are not one-off tendencies, but habitual decision-making characteristics of the human condition. So worrying is the proven manifestations of confirmation bias that Nickerson opens the article by writing:

> If one were to attempt to identify a single problematic aspect of human reasoning that deserves attention above all others, the confirmation bias would have to be among the candidates for consideration.[27]

And on the validity of the results, Nickerson quotes another author, Evans: 'Confirmation bias is perhaps the best known and most widely accepted notion of inferential error to come out of the literature on human reasoning .'[28]

Of course, psychology is not the only domain where defective human reasoning has been studied and catalogued: The economic sciences have been increasingly interested in economic decision making under controlled conditions, finding numerous examples of irrational human behaviour;[29] studies on climate science find great divergence between scientific consensus and public understanding,[30] whilst to historians, bias is *a fact of life*. There is nothing contentious about the assertion that all sources are influenced by the author's world-view. The working methodology of the historian is to first identify the bias, and then try to uncover the historical 'truth' lying beneath (or between) the various biased accounts of an event or time.

A summary

To this point we have met the world-view (or presuppositional) hypothesis as a way to understand the underlying differences between participants in a theistic-atheist dialogue. Moreover, we have seen that this hypothesis is consistent with, or rather arises from, the biblical narrative. Unsurprisingly, the hypothesis is confirmed by empirical studies and is an assumed feature of several branches of academic inquiry that concern human decision-making. All of which leaves us, perhaps, with an even stronger feeling of disillusionment with the prospects for our dialoguing scientists' clashing 'ideological universes'.

We might rightly ask again: *Why bother?* If world-views are so deeply set in the heart and mind of a person, if they are so tightly held, if they direct not just the faculties of reasoning but even the data on which those faculties will work, why make any effort to build a bridge between world-views?

At the outset I insisted that this was an optimistic piece. Let me now show why.

Making progress: why dialogue is still worthwhile

The two authors that we have met repeatedly in this essay thus far, John M Frame and James Sire, each have their own reasons to be optimistic. I encourage the reader to consider these arguments.

Frame notes that whilst the problem of 'non-overlapping philosophical stadia' might be impossible for two non-Christians (for all of the reasons we have seen above), the prospects are radically different for Christians dialoguing across the fence. I will paraphrase three of his points here and add my own in conclusion:

i. Because all men 'know God'

First, returning to our arguments above, the biblical testimony is that all people 'know God'; they know Him because they are born in his image,[31] and because he has 'clearly' revealed himself to them in the 'things that have been created'.[32] Whilst it is true that the unregenerate man suppresses this truth, the Christian can appeal to a 'memory of that revelation'.[33] This argument echoes the writer of Ecclesiastes, where '[God] has put eternity into man's heart, yet so that he cannot find out what God has done from the beginning to the end'. (Ecc 3:11) Humanity at once 'knows God', yet does not know him. Yet the Bible teaches us that in every man's heart is a remnant of that knowledge—his true identity under God. This, the Christian can appeal to. Of this deeper level, Frame writes:

> At that level, he knows that empiricism is wrong and that scripture's standards are right. We direct our apologetic witness not to his empiricist epistemology or whatever, but to his memory of God's revelation and to the epistemology implicit in that revelation.[34]

ii. Because the gospel never goes out alone

Second, as we have already seen, whilst scripture in general, and the gospel in particular, work to divide the very heart of man, the gospel is itself made powerful for salvation by the work of the Holy Spirit. Or in Frame's words 'our witness to the unbeliever never comes alone'.[35] God's promise to the ambassador for Christ is that her appeal will come with the 'power of God and the wisdom of God' on those who are to believe.[36] Here, is the dramatic, remarkable, and graciously regenerative power of God, which can speak from one ideological universe into another. And not just in a casual or informal way like so much chatter, but in a life-transforming, *leave-everything-behind* clarion call of salvation.

iii. Because God has given various ways to communicate the gospel

Having said that it is 'the message (not the medium) that is the message', there are still various ways to tell the same message. Indeed, God has given a great diversity of presentations of the same central truth throughout His word. Part of 'speaking across the void' is to recognise that, just as all men can be said to 'know God', all men are formed as embodied human beings—we are not mere vessels for a spirit or soul. We are each individually formed with our own particular characteristics, history, scars, successes and interests.[37] What communicates effectively to one person may be fuzzy and incoherent to another.

For instance, if an 'evidential' argument on the historicity of Jesus seems to fail, one could switch to a more 'offensive' approach, asking questions of the other about their world-view, identifying inconsistencies, appealing to principles of internal consistency or 'making-sense' of the world around us (Sire's seven questions would be a good starting point); or one could share a parable from the Gospels of Jesus, which was the Old Testament prophets' and Jesus's own favoured method for speaking to the heart of his hearers (e.g. Nathan to David in 2 Sam 11, 12, 'You are that man!'; or Matt 13, the 'Parable of The Sower').

God's *dramatis personae* revealed in His word demonstrate a creativity and richness matching the creativity and richness of the creation itself.

Such examples should push the Christian to a deeper knowledge of the scriptures, not only for his or her own maturity, but to taste and see for themselves the multifaceted gospel prism that illumines, convicts and transforms God's people.

Finally, as with Frame's forceful comment we saw earlier, the New Testament doesn't leave the Christian with a sense that proclaiming Jesus is optional. Indeed, the Apostle Paul writes to the Corinthians,

> For the love of Christ controls us, because we have concluded this: that one has died for all, therefore all have died; and he died for all, that those who live might no longer live for themselves but for him who for their sake died and was raised.[38]

For the Apostle, Christ's love is *all-controlling*; following Christ is not a Sunday-only activity, nor an *only-when-others-are-watching* persona, it is the all-controlling mindset and orientation of the heart that presses in on every aspect, action, thought and emotion of the believer. It arises from a conclusion that a believer's life is given over to Christ ('enslaved', cf. Rom 6:20-22), that her former life of rebellion has been put to death at the cross, and now, she lives life as a 'new creation .. the old has passed away; behold, the new has come' (II Cor 5:17).

Ultimately, just as there is no neutrality on the matter of world-views, there is no middle-ground for the believer. The supremacy of Christ's Lordship is *the* primary pre-commitment for the believer; the ministry of reconciliation our every-day appeal to all whom God brings into our life (cf. II Cor 5:18-21).

---

[1] See: http://www.venganza.org/, 'The Church of the Flying Spaghetti Monster' is a parody atheist 'religion'.

[2] Here, I'm loosely channeling Richard Dawkins and John Lennox, who recently debated 'The God Delusion'. See: http://fixed-point.org/index.php/video/35-full-length/164-the-dawkins-lennox-debate.

[3] J. W. Sire, *The Universe Next Door* 4th ed., (Downers Grove, IL, InterVarsity Press, 2004), 20.

[4] Sire, *Naming the Elephant*, (Downers Grove, IL IVP Academic. 2004), 23.

[5] Sire, *The Universe Next Door*, 17.

[6] Ibid., 20, or Sire, *Naming the Elephant*, 20.

[7] J. M. Frame, *Apologetics to the Glory of God*, (Phillipsburg: P & R Publishing, 1994), 6.

[8] Frame, *Apologetics to the Glory of God*, 8.

[9] Sire, *Naming the Elephant*, 21.

[10] D.A. Carson, 'Must I learn to interpret the Bible', *The Briefing*, 253 (2000): 11-14.

[11] 1 Cor 1:18.

[12] Lk 12:51.

[13] 1 Cor 2:2.

[14] 1 Cor 2:13-14.

[15] 1 Cor 2:1.

[16] Heb 4:12.

[17] Gen 3.

[18] Rom 1:19-25, cf. Ps 19.

[19] Rom 1:21.

[20] Rom 1:18.

[21] Rom 1:25.

[22] cf. Jn 1:10-11

[23] Col 1:15-18

[24] Jn 1:1-5

[25] Frame, *Apologetics to the Glory of God*, 9.

[26] R. S. Nickerson, 'Confirmation bias: A ubiquitous phenomenon in many guises'. *Review of General Psychology* 2, no. 2, (1998): 175–220.

[27] Ibid., 175.

[28] Ibid.

[29] C. F. Camerer & R. H. Thaler, 'Anomalies: Ultimatums, Dictators and Manners'. *The Journal of Economic Perspectives* 9, no. 2 (1995): 209–219.

[30] J. D. Sterman, (2011). Communicating Climate Change Risks. *Climatic Change*, no. 108 (2011): 811–826.

[31] Gen 1,2.

[32] Rom 1:20.

[33] Frame, *Apologetics to the Glory of God*, 11.

[34] Ibid.

[35] Ibid. cf. Rom 15:18-19.

[36] 1 Cor 1:22-25.

[37] Cf. Ps 139, Acts 17:22ff.

[38] 2 Cor 5:14-15.

Chapter 3: Why Atheists Worry about Believers...
and what believers can learn from that

Greg Restall

There are atheists, and there are the *New Atheists*. In the marketplace of ideas and ideologies, some atheists are content to hold their views to themselves while others share their atheism with the fervour of the keenest evangelist. We shouldn't expect it to be any other way: after all, there are quiet religious believers, and there are religious believers who are keen to share their enthusiasms with others. But the fervour of the New Atheism of Dawkins, Harris and Hitchens carries a distinctive edge. Their passion is not just that atheism is a good thing, to be shared and promulgated. It's that belief in God is positively and actively bad. Not just wrong-headed or incorrect. It's dangerous.

I am interested in this phenomenon: What does this mean for those of us who believe? What can we learn from the reactions of these smart men? (These New Atheists in the popular sphere are, by and large, men.) It is often when we take a sympathetic eye to others' perspective, listen, and attempt to understand their views and concerns, that we can learn things. In the case of the New Atheists, I think that we can see something new about ourselves, about what belief in God actually means, what it could mean for us, and perhaps a little more about what it should mean for us, too. I hope that the upshot will be increased understanding all round, not just increased understanding of what others believe and why, but also of ourselves, and of our place in God's world.

So, what can we learn about the intensity of the opposition of the New Atheists? Whatever it signifies, it's not just that theists are *wrong*. It's that we're dangerously wrong. It would be an advance for the world to be rid of theism in all its forms. This shouldn't be a big surprise: after all, many believers think that it would be better for the world to be rid of atheism, or incorrect religious belief in all its forms, and many supporters of sporting teams flirt with the idea that it would be better if there were fewer or no supporters of rival teams.

In any disagreement like this, opposition can take positive and negative forms. The positive form is that of the generous sharing of a gift: I have learned something about the world and our place in it and I want to share it with you. Learning that there is no God has liberated me from false consciousness, and I would like for you to experience the same joy, satisfaction and insight that it brings! We see this in a little of the evangelistic fervour of Dawkins' introduction to science for kids: *The Magic of Reality.*[1] This book is not merely a neutral introduction to the wonders of science. It's also a positive, and largely winsome exposition of science as the comprehensive way that we come to know anything and everything. Dawkins has found truth and liberation (or at least, what he takes to be true and liberating) and he is keen to share that gift with us.

That is the positive form of the opposition, and in a world where people take different perspectives on issues of importance, it is to be expected, and frankly, to be celebrated. Imagine a world where we all attempted to constructively share what was good in our perspectives, our views, and our traditions—where believers of all stripes tried to outdo each other in positively presenting their own views and celebrated what was good and true and beautiful, and where we all sought out what truth and goodness and beauty we could find. There would be much in a world like this that we could enjoy.

However, this is not the world we are in here and now. People aren't like that, and not all presentations of different views are motivated by a desire to share what is true and good.

Much of the opposition to religious belief from the New Atheists takes a harder edge. It isn't just the enthusiasm of someone with good news to share. The *wrongness* the New Atheists perceive in believers is not just the wrongness of simple matters of fact. It's not like we're just missing some fact that others can plainly see, though there is an element of this in the New Atheists' criticism. It is not the kind of regrettable blindness in those who cannot perceive what is good in some genre of art or any other kind of aesthetic appreciation. We are not merely criticised for lacking taste or being tone deaf. Instead, the opposition in the atheism of Hitchens's *God Is Not Great*[2] (to take just one example), is the opposition that takes theism to be genuinely and worryingly *dangerous*.

For the New Atheists, theism—whatever form it takes—is fundamentally dangerous and destructive. It is dangerous not merely because of any accidental features it has, but it is essentially dangerous because of the kind of belief it is. Belief in God is a totalising, all-encompassing view. Theism takes in *all* of life. It has implications for everything, for how we are to view the world, for how we are to understand what is right and wrong, and for how we are to run our society. According to the New Atheists, we theists are wrong—deeply, importantly, and dangerously wrong.

So, opposition between theists and atheists is more like the kind of opposition between proponents of radically different political views, such as fascists and communists. In its starkest form, each takes the other to be to not just wrong, but to be illegitimate and dangerous—a force to be opposed on all fronts and at all times. We can never have common cause and never even find a comfortable middle ground. Our view puts us beyond the pale to our opponents.

For the New Atheists, the illegitimacy of theism takes a number of forms. Our illegitimacy can be a matter of truth and knowledge and reason—it can be an *epistemic* failing. Many of us, to be sure, hold beliefs without good reason. Probably all of us, whether theists or atheists, let our ideas outrun our evidence. That may be dangerous enough, but in the early 21st Century, the worry is not just at the level of a clash of ideas. The concern is political. For the New Atheists, we believers are dangerous when it comes to politics, to organising our life together. Many theists not only propose dangerous social changes, but have the power to enact them. We are dangerous to have around in the body politic. From the repressive religious regimes of history, present-day Islamic fundamentalism of the Middle East, to the restrictions on personal liberties in some states of the

USA, religious believers have put their mark on political life in many unacceptable ways. For the New Atheists, this isn't just an accident. It reveals our true nature, and it shows why religious belief is dangerous and should be stopped.

The natural response for a believer is to be defensive and to immediately deny, to backpedal, or to point to positive examples of religious believers who have been a force for good in the world. This is easy enough to do, and there are many good examples to which we can point. But let's not do this. Pause for a moment and sit with the critique. Might there not be something correct here for us to listen to? Is there something in the nature of belief in God that has this tendency to dominate and control? Is there something in the religious narrative that is totalising in just this way? Our religious traditions call for submission in all of life, in the whole world. This is easier to see when we look at religious believers from traditions other than our own. Do *we* ever see the committed believer from another tradition as dangerous? That is how all believers can be seen to those outside *any* tradition.

So, what can we take away and learn from this critique? Is it a case where we should simply wear the badge with pride and accept that the unbeliever—or the believer from another tradition—will find us dangerous, and simply celebrate it, or take it as a mark of genuine belief? Or does this outsider's view of belief in God show up deeper underlying issues?

I think that the critique of religious views as totalising and dangerous does point to something important, and I think that the critique of the New Atheists of religious believers actually points to a sense in which many religious believers are (as a matter of fact) not radical *enough* in our religious belief. The theist thinks that there is a God. The Christian believes that this God is revealed to all humanity in Jesus Christ. The evangelical Christian believes that this story of Jesus is given to us in scripture. This seems at face value to be a very dangerous view, and a very immodest belief with implications for all of life, demanding total allegiance. Yet, there is another sense in which this view is dangerously *modest* and *de-centring* for the believer. Let me explain how.

If I have learned anything in placing my faith in God, it is that I am not at the centre of the universe. I am not even at the centre of *my* world. To believe in God—and this is something that is common to many traditions and expressions of belief in God—we submit to something other than ourselves. It is not for nothing that *pride* or self-centredness is taken to be a deadly sin in many traditions, and it is not for nothing that *idolatry*— taking something other than God, something we can manufacture or control—to be God, is a continual temptation. To say that *God* is truly at the centre of the universe, and not ourselves or anything to which *we* have prior ownership, has very many radical consequences for our thought and our practice. That God is God and that we are not means that we do not *know* everything. Our view is not to be identified as God's view. We see only in part. And since everyone *else* is also in God's world—since God truly exists and is at the centre and the ground of the whole world, and is not just a private affair for me, and since God's Spirit is active in the whole world and not just here and with me or my people, I have something, at least potentially, to learn from everyone. To genuinely believe that this is God's universe and not mine alone is to be open to God's work and God's truth from anywhere and everywhere. We are to test the spirits, of course, and we are to hold fast to what is good from wherever it comes. Belief in God, if it is not to be an idolatry where we identify God with our own current view of what God is like, can lead us to be open to what we can learn from others, both modest enough to know that we won't know all of the answers, and confident and trusting that we can share with others what we have learned to be true.

So, what does this mean for the New Atheist critique and for our response?

On the plane of our *knowledge* about the world and whether our religious belief is reasonable, we can admit that some believers have better reasons for their beliefs than others: Some come to belief though being convinced with an argument; others through a direct encounter with Jesus; yet others absorb belief through the faith being handed down through the generations. If there really is a God, then belief will be acquired in many different ways: in the same way that people come to know some or other aspect of the world through a mix of direct experience, hearsay or testimony and active research. The quality of that information is not just a matter for the individual, but also for the community at large. In the case of belief in God, it is up to *us*, the believing community, to get things as right as we can make them, to understand God and our relationship to God as best we can, and to share that understanding in as clear a way as we can. This will always be tempered with the knowledge that it's not that *we* have privileged access to God, which cannot be shared by everyone else. If God is the God of the entire universe, then God can speak to all, reveal himself to all. Wherever we go, God's Spirit was there first. If we think—as we should—that God is specially revealed to us in Jesus, then we must be very careful to remember that it is not our own idea of God that we are to worship (that would be idolatry). It is the God who is revealed in Jesus, and who created the entire world that we are to worship. Again, there is an external authority to which we submit, beyond ourselves. It follows that we must be careful of our own views, to learn to listen as well as to speak, and to be a good conversation partner. This will mean that we will not only help others, but we will also learn new things for ourselves. If there truly is a God, then we can trust that God will use our contributions in the lives of those around us, and we do not have to be so anxious to think that it is *merely* up to us to convince those we meet. If God is at work in the world, then it is our joyful task to be a part of that work, and we can rest in the knowledge that God can take up our efforts and use them to his purposes.

What, then, of the perceived political danger of belief in God? If we were to genuinely believe in God, how are believers to act in the political sphere? Are we a danger to those who disagree with us? At the very least, we should remember that if there is a God, he values each person as his own, and that however I treat another human being, whether one of my tradition who agrees with me or one whose views are radically opposed to mine, this is a person who God loves and cares for. All that I do to another being is answerable to God. So, however we are to arrange ourselves in our life together in the community, it cannot be just by imposing our will without regard for the interests or views of others. It is one thing to think that understanding who God is and what God wants gives us some insight into what is good and bad for human society; it is another to say that any of those views are to be imposed without due consideration. In all things we are to treat others as we would be treated ourselves. Christian faith started out in a minority community, where the proponents acted by persuasion, by living a life of example, by service to the poor and needy. It would do us well to act in that way in the future, for then we would not only be doing good for those around us, but the *way* we acted in the political sphere would show the same care and concern as we believe God has shown us.

The New Atheists worry that religious belief is radical and dangerous. This is true, but their worry points to a way in which our belief is *not radical enough*. If we take seriously the idea that God is at the centre of our world and not us, then we will not attempt to use God as a mark of some partisan perspective, but we will show the true humility and service we have been shown in Jesus. This is the real implication of the belief that there is a God—it is not ever true to say that God is *our* God, as if we could possess him and impose him on others. It is much more true to say that we are God's. If Christians were to think and act in this way, then the reaction of our atheist brothers and sisters, I dare say, would sound very different.

---

[1] Richard Dawkins (author) and Dave McKean (illustrator), *The Magic of Reality*, (New York: Free Press, 2011).
[2] Christopher Hitchens, *God Is Not Great*, (New York: 12/Warner Books, 2007).

Chapter 4: God the Intimate Interventionist:

Nick Cave and Dietrich Bonhoeffer in dialogue

Gordon Preece

Nick Cave, the great Australian gothic rock artist, writes songs that are God-bothering and bothered. But his most popular song is best-known for its negative line 'I don't believe in an interventionist God'. Along with REM's *Losing My Religion*, it is the anthem for many a New Atheist. Many Christians, ever-defensive and alert against the New Atheists mistakenly quote Cave in this way. Tragically, Christians' tone-deafness highlights the way we are so often distracted by the angry New Atheists from addressing the anguished longing of those who Charles Taylor in *A Secular Age*[1] describes as 'cross-pressured': unbelievers aware that the rumour of God kept alive by billions can't be easily dismissed; believers aware there are many unbelievers with good reason for being so, finding echoes in the chamber of their own hearts on dark and silent nights. Cave, a God-wrestler if ever there was one, goes on to sing of his lover, 'but darlin' I know you do' and then prayerfully hymn God in the resounding refrain 'into my arms O Lord, into my arms'. To understand what Cave means by this impassioned cry to the Intimate Interventionist we need to set this song about his muse in the context of the long journey of Cave's God-haunted musical musings. We also need to draw him into dialogue with Dietrich Bonhoeffer, from his prison cell in Berlin (a place formative for Cave's own music), anxiously awaiting a possible reunion with his young fiancé. This great theological critic of faith in a 'God of the gaps', an abstract transcendence, a pious religiousness, sees it as a cover-up for our follies, failures and childish irresponsibilities.

Australian literary scholars Peter Conrad and Lyn McCredden have recently written about Cave's gruesome gothic spirituality, grappling with the paradoxical absence and presence of God. In *The Good Son*,[2] Conrad writes as one who doesn't 'expect to see the face of God'[3] and sees religion as 'a metaphysical exercise in killing, since God created the world only to have the pleasure of slowly destroying it'.[4] Drawing on Cave's music, art works, writings and films he couches Cave in a neo-Freudian psychological perspective. Cave 'often impersonates a pinioned Christ, writhing in excruciation',[5] seeking absolution from his late father, an English teacher who endowed him with his love of literature and scripture. His father's 1978 death in a car crash was conveyed to Cave and his mother at St. Kilda police station where she was literally bailing him out from a charge of drunken vandalism. In a sense he's always been on bail, never acquitted from the 'abject horror' of this pivotal episode. This plays itself out in the visceral violence of Cave's lyrics and images. For Conrad 'Cave has spent three decades begging pardon for an Oedipal crime he didn't actually commit, while punishing the world for its random injustice by fancifully killing off everyone who isn't his irreplaceable father'.[6]

But there is a more positive side of what Conrad sees as Cave's primal patriarchal projection onto 'God'. Speaking on love songs Cave states: 'The loss of my father created in my life a vacuum, a space in which my words began to float and collect and find their purpose',[7] art setting its face against Ecclesiastes 'vanity of vanities'. The sin and sorrow of life 'under the sun' that Cave's similar capacity for melancholy takes so seriously, is epitomised in his felt complicity in his father's death.

Conrad's psychological interpretation is readily understandable and its pivotal place in his pilgrimage both toward and away from God provokes an insightful but ultimately reductionist reading of Cave. For him, Cave is aptly named, prophetically preferring the gloom and darkness of caves while awaiting 'the darkness that will descend on us all', to the preferred Australian narrative of prophets coming from the desert. Cave abhors 'Australia, where the sun shines', in his 1999 lecture on love songs. Conrad sums up:

> Cave's grudges and rages and festering vendettas made him an artist, and his despair and hatred made him a believer; at this late hour he is exactly the kind of rankling conscience the world needs. Although I don't ever expect to see the face of God, I imagine that if he did exist, he

> might have a face like Cave's – scarily sombre, with an adamantine gaze
> and a mouth that twitches to hint at a sense of humour as black as his
> hair.[8]

Conrad's tragic tale finally finds hints of hope in Cave's black undertaker
humour, a figure Cave sartorially imitates.

However, while taking Cave's dark side as seriously as Conrad, I will
argue that there is more hope available here, drawing on McCredden and
Bonhoeffer. To my mind Conrad's preference for cave imagery provides
a platonic view of Cave, where unchanging spiritual reality is preferenced
over the physical shadows dancing on the walls of the cave in Plato's
famous allegory. In fact, this very dichotomy, dominating neo-platonic
Western Christianity since Augustine, gives us the isolated, interfering,
'interventionist God', the absentee landlord that Cave and many of his
contemporaries disbelieve. McCredden provides us with a more
integrated reading of Cave which is not only tragic and cruciform, but
comedic, incarnational and resurrectional in its view of embodied love.
Ironically, Conrad quotes Cave's *Wild World*, but misses its
resurrectional implications: 'Hold me up, baby, Cave begs. 'Our bodies
melt together (we are one)/Post crucifixion, baby'.[9]

McCredden's *The Carnal Theologies of Nick Cave*[10] rightly questions the
way twentieth century anthropologists and religious historians like
Mircea Eliade in his *The Sacred and the Profane*, opposed the two
domains. By contrast, 'Cave's sacred, is deeply enmeshed in the human
dimensions of flesh, erotics, and violence'.[11] Cave critiques the bloodless
Christianity of much of the church, but craves tangible communion with
God. In *Brompton Oratory* (on *The Boatman's Call* album), he longs for
the recognition of the resurrected Christ as he 'returns to his loved ones'
in the reading from Luke 24, but is not unfeeling like the stone apostles
looking down, longing for 'a beauty impossible … the blood imparted in
little sips/the smell of you still on my hands/as I bring the cup up to my
lips'. This incarnational intimacy and rejection of an impassive, externally
interventionist God is captured in the last verse 'No God up in the sky,
/No devil beneath the sea, /Could do the job that you did, baby/ of

bringing me to my knees'. Here, human and divine desire mingle, in body and blood, in what for many might seem blasphemous, but then so they said of the Incarnation.

It was the great Christian poet Francis Thompson who sadly said 'I cannot see the Glory, for the colour of her hair'. But Cave is a better, more biblical poet in seeing the glory in the colour of her hair or her smell on his hands. There is good precedent for this: the medieval English wedding service (and the Sydney Anglican service) has a vow where the man promises 'I worship you with my body'. And the medieval wife earthily promises 'to be buxom in bed and in board'! I once wrote a poem to my wife after the birth of our third child where I knelt and 'worshipped' her with my body.

This brings us to the magnificent *Into My Arms*, from *The Boatman's Call* again. The album title recalls Charon, the mythical boatman of the final watery journey to the underworld. It provides the dark background that lets the love song shine brighter. As I noted the famous first line 'I don't believe in an interventionist God' has deafened many Christians to its deeper desires. They miss its 'Lord, I believe, help my unbelief' tension – beautifully capturing the cross-pressured nature of contemporary secularity. But Cave goes on: 'But if I did I would kneel down and ask Him/ Not to intervene when it came to you/ Not to touch a hair on your head/ To leave you as you are/ And if He felt He had to direct you/ Then direct you into my arms'. This humorous 'doubter's dialogue' with Cave's believing better half turns serious with the prayerful plea to light her journey back, to constantly return her 'into my arms, O Lord' so they may 'walk like Christ, in grace and love'. Underneath his arms, the lover trusts, 'are the everlasting arms' (Deut 33:27).[12] This is indeed an intimate interventionist.

A less ambiguous conviction of and desire for a tangible, palpable presence comes through even more clearly in the 'thoroughgoing kind of incarnationalism'[13] of *There Is A Kingdom* from the same album: 'There is a kingdom, /There is a king, /And he lives without /And he lives within /And he is everything'. Later in *Gates of the Garden*, on the 2001 album

No More Shall We Meet Cave feels echoes of Eden in the living, breathing vitality of erotic engagement 'as we open up the gates of the garden'. And like the intimacy of 'Into My Arms', 'God is in this hand that I hold'.[14] We should beware though, lest we lose sight of the tightrope Cave walks, of the tensions within his texts, nor try to make them too theologically precise rather than erotically evocative. As McCredden sums up so well, 'redemption is imagined by Cave, but rarely without the accompanying shadows of uncertainty'[15] and violence, as in his script and musical score of the 2005 film of Australian frontier violence, *The Proposition*.[16]

Yet the intervention of God's kingdom is captured well in Cave's riveting introduction to Mark's Gospel in the Canongate series of biblical books. Cave gets Mark's sense of immediacy, often conveyed by Mark's regular repetition of the Greek *euthus*–usually translated 'immediately', which gives the rapid-fire sense of the urgency of the kingdom's coming, just around the bend. But Cave stops short of the ultimate intervention of the resurrection, albeit Mark's is the most ambiguous and mysterious version of the empty tomb, met by the fear of the women finding it. Cave may not be, yet, an orthodox Christian, but his captivation with Christ shows he is not far from the kingdom. Perhaps a dialogue with a kindred spirit like Bonhoeffer might close any gap.

As a segue to Bonhoeffer's nuanced notion of divine 'intervention', the normally sophisticated English comedian Eddie Izzard activates the stereotype of the interventionist God in the context of Nazi Germany. In his recent live DVD *Stripped* he raises the post-Holocaust question of Emerson, Lake and Palmer as to 'Why did He [God] lose six million Jews?' Izzard says: 'Hitler was saying "I will kill them all, burn them in the ovens". That's enough of a hint to knock his head off, time for a bit of divine intervention don't you think?'

But Bonhoeffer, in his intimate letters to best friend and confessor Eberhard Bethge, was never one to rely on the *Deus ex machina* or God of the gaps, the machine that the Greek dramatists would turn on or off when they needed a neat resolution to the ragged, torn tragedies of history. Bonhoeffer resisted such easy resolutions, resolutely holding to his and others' human responsibility to act, with enormous risk, against the human tyrannies the term 'tragedy' tends to fatalistically hide. God is a God of the centre, not of the borders or the gaps.[17]

This is why Bonhoeffer wrote out of his sense of separation from his fiancé Maria to his friend facing separation from his wife Renate and first child Dietrich:

> In the first place nothing can fill the gap when we are away from those we love, and it would be wrong to try and find anything. We must simply hold out and win through. That sounds very hard at first, but at the same time it is a great consolation, since leaving the gap unfilled preserves the bonds between us. It is nonsense to say that God fills the gap: he does not fill it, but keeps it empty so that our communion with another may be kept alive, even at the cost of pain.[18]

Bonhoeffer wrote that new year about his determination to see life not from his privileged position nor from that of a metaphysically detached and transcendent God who could be treated as a tool to reinforce our view 'from above'.

> There remains an experience of incomparable value. We have for once learnt to see the great events of history from below, from the perspective of the outcast, the suspects, the maltreated, the powerless, the oppressed, the reviled - in short from the perspective of those who suffer ... This perspective from below must not become the particular possession of those who are eternally dissatisfied; rather, we must do justice to life in all its dimensions from a higher satisfaction, whose foundation is beyond any talk of, "from below" or "from above." This is the way in which we may affirm it.[19]

This transcendence is not a religious form of cheap and quick compensation for the weak and 'eternally dissatisfied' whose manipulative slave morality Nietzsche despised; it is neither classical, dualistic metaphysics nor pietistic inwardness and individualism;[20] 'it is at once both a worldly and a spiritual transcendence' fit for humans in their strength and 'coming of age'.

On 21 July, 1944, the day after the failed plot to assassinate Hitler, Bonhoeffer wrote in a way that connects to Cave's metaphor, of 'throwing oneself completely into the arms of God' identifying with 'the suffering of God in the world ... awake with Christ in Gethsemane'.[21] We are called to be on the side of suffering humanity, as Jesus 'the man for others' was, in a form of this-worldly transcendence or intimate intervention.

In Bonhoeffer's *Ethics* and *Letters* this earthy transcendence or 'religionless Christianity' involves the more subtle intervention of an improvisational ethics of radical responsibility. It is found in following the 'man for others' in the otherly, awe-inspiring, aesthetic transcendence of this worldly encounter with human faces and earthly realities. This aesthetic awakening opened Bonhoeffer to a polyphonic and multi-dimensional faith. Bonhoeffer celebrated its multiplicity in a letter to a distressed Bethge on 20 May 1944.

> There is always a danger of intense love destroying what I might call the 'polyphony' of life. What I mean is that God requires that we should love him eternally with our whole hearts, yet not so as to compromise or diminish our earthly affections, but as a kind of *cantus firmus* to which the other melodies of life provide a counterpoint. Earthly affection is one of these contrapuntal themes, a theme which enjoys an autonomy of its own. Even the Bible can find room for the Song of Songs, and one could hardly have a more passionate and sensual love than is there portrayed ... it is a good thing that that book is included in the Bible as a protest against those who believe that the Bible stands for the restraint of passion (is there any example of such restraint anywhere in the Old Testament? [which may explain its deep attraction to Cave and Bonhoeffer]). Where the ground bass is firm and clear, there is nothing to stop the counterpoint from being developed to the utmost of its limits. Both ground bass and counterpoint are 'without confusion and yet distinct', in the words of the Chalcedon formula, like Christ in his divine and human natures. Perhaps the importance of polyphony in music lies in the fact that it is a musical reflection of this Christological truth, and ... therefore an essential element in the Christian life. All this hadn't occurred to me till after you were here. Can you see what I'm driving at? I wanted to tell you that we must have a good,

clear *cantus firmus*. Without it there can be no full or perfect sound, but with it the counterpoint has a firm support and cannot get out of tune or fade out, yet is always a perfect or distinct whole in its own right. ... Only a polyphony of this kind can give life a wholeness, and at the same time assure us that nothing [calamitous] can go wrong so long as the *cantus firmus* is kept going.... Perhaps your leave and the separation which lies ahead will be easier for you to bear. Please do not fear or hate separation a good deal will be easier to bear in these days together, and possibly also in the days ahead when you are separated. Please, [Eberhard], do not fear and hate the separation, if it should come again, with all its attendant perils, but rely on the *cantus firmus*.[22]

The next day, May 21, Bonhoeffer wrote: 'The subject of polyphony is still pursuing me. I was thinking to-day how painful it is without you, and it occurred to me how pain and joy are also part of the polyphony of life, and that they can exist independently side by side.'[23]

Here Bonhoeffer develops an aesthetic, incarnational theology of persons and love, based on the classical musical principle of the *cantus firmus* that he knew well as a concert level pianist. 'A *cantus firmus* is a melody to which one or more contrapuntal parts can be added—parts that are truly distinct, novel and even seemingly at odds with other parts until they are bound to this consistent yet fluid melody that is the *cantus firmus*.'[24] Bonhoeffer extends the musical analogy to Christ's two natures, divine and human, which join, without fusing or destroying, divine and human love. The intimacy of the incarnation links divine and human life and love, through the membrane of Christ's manhood or humanity. To link this with Bonhoeffer's *Ethics,* it means that the penultimate or natural sphere of human loves is not annihilated by the ultimate, divine love, but nature is preserved and perfected by grace, not through a more distant divinity, or generic 'God-ness', but in the particular person of Jesus Christ, the very definition of the natural, of life and love.

Jeremy Begbie's book *Resounding Truth: Christian Wisdom in the World of Music*[25] gets Bonhoeffer's gist. Bonhoeffer, he says:

Envisages a polyphonous kind of life for the church in the world, a rich life shot through with joy.... It is a life of 'worldliness' – not the worldliness of the secularist, denying God, nor the worldliness of a certain kind of aesthete, fleeing responsibility, but a fully down-to-earth kind of Christian life that can include free, 'aesthetic existence' (friendship, art, etc.) while also being ethically alert and responsible.

Bonhoeffer here takes the good and beautiful as seriously as the true in Plato's great trilogy. By his aesthetic turn and musical terms he is able to break through the poverty of much religious 'interventionist' language in a way that respects the relative autonomy of the created realm and relationships. God is not only expressed in modernistic-style factual propositions, (as former Moore College Principal Broughton Knox's 'Propositional Revelation, the Only Revelation' claimed), but God also propositions and woos us.

The musical turn as fellow classical pianist-theologian Begbie recognises, gets us beyond the literal dis-place-ment of God in modernity, with its dominant use of spatial analogies, as if the square peg of abstract divinity cannot fit in the round hole of humanity. At his 2010 New College University of NSW lectures, he would play a note, and then another, each distinct, but harmonious entities. They did not engulf each other, as in the modern view of generic divinity and humanity, but in their joined particularity in the incarnation, co-exist, bringing the best out in each other. As Bonhoeffer's theological mentor Karl Barth once said, God doesn't have to make humanity small to make himself big.

Bonhoeffer is perhaps literally closest to Cave's *Into My Arms* on December 18, 1943, writing that:

> To long for the transcendent when you are in your wife's arms is, to put it mildly, a lack of taste, and it is certainly not what God expects of us. We ought to find God and love him in the blessings he sends us. If he pleases to grant us some overwhelming earthly bliss, we ought not to try and be more religious than God himself.... Once a man has found God in his earthly bliss and has thanked him for it, there will be plenty of opportunities to remind himself that these earthly pleasures are only

transitory, and that it is good to accustom himself to the idea of eternity... But everything in its season, and the important thing is to keep in step with God, and not to get a step or two in front of him (nor for that matter, a step or two behind him either). It is arrogant to want to have everything at once—matrimonial bliss, and the cross, and the heavenly Jerusalem, where there is no longer marriage, nor giving in marriage. 'To everything there is a season' (Ecclesiastes 3). Everything has its time ... a time to embrace, and a time to refrain from embracing ... and God seeketh again that which is passed away.'[26]

Bonhoeffer here understands the essence of the enigmatic Ecclesiastes. Not the common platonic dualist, despairing translation and interpretation of Ecclesiastes' view of 'vanity' as a modern form of existentialist 'meaninglessness' or futility, but the advocate of enjoyment of each moment of pleasure as a blessing and gift from God, not forever, but for now.

But Bonhoeffer also rightly wrestles with the meaning of the last verse of Ecclesiastes 3 refracted through one of his favourite hymns and a solid, earthy sense of biblical eschatology, not today's common escapology. He writes to Bethge:

Nothing is lost, everything is taken up again in Christ, ... transfigured in the process, becoming transparent, clear and free from all self-seeking and desire. Christ brings it all again as God intended it to be.... The doctrine of the restoration of all things ... which is derived from Ephesians 1:10, recapitulation (Irenaeus), is a magnificent conception, and full of comfort. This is the way in which the words 'God seeketh again that which is passed away' are fulfilled. [27]

Again Bonhoeffer is helped by music, a line from the Augustinian *O bone Jesu* by Schutz.

Is not this phrase [O good Jesus], with its combination of ecstatic longing and transparent devotion, suggestive of the restoration of all earthly desire? Restoration of course must not be confused with sublimation, for sublimation is sarx [flesh] (and pietistic?!), and restoration 'spirit', not in the sense of spiritualisation, ... but as ... a new creation, through the Holy Spirit.[28]

In the end, Cave's craving for his lover, his carnal desire to cradle her in his arms, is sanctified by the in-carn-ate One of the cradle, cross, resurrection and consummation. The God of the Incarnation, is, as Bonhoeffer knew well, while longing for his bride-to-be beyond the prison walls, an intimate interventionist. This intimacy and subtlety, making space for even the most horrific human evil, means that God did not intervene to save Bonhoeffer from the Nazis. But as Scott Holland notes nicely concerning Bonhoeffer's hanging on April 9, 1945: 'I would like to think that in the end, in the dark beauty of worldly holiness, for Bonhoeffer, *the Infinite and the intimate became one*'.[29]   In Bonhoeffer's own words approaching the gallows, and the everlasting arms, for me 'this is the beginning of life' in even greater intimacy, face to face, knowing as he was already known.

---

[1] Charles Taylor, *A Secular Age* (Boston: Belknap, 2007), ch. 16
[2] Peter Conrad, 'The Good Son', *The Monthly* August (2009): 28-37.
[3] Ibid., 37.
[4] Ibid., 28.
[5] Ibid., 30.
[6] Ibid., 35.
[7] Ibid., 31.
[8] Ibid., 37.
[9] Ibid., 30.
[10] Lyn McCredden, 'The Carnal Theologies of Nick Cave' in *Luminous Moments* (Adelaide: ATF Press, 2010).
[11] Ibid., 105.
[12] Ibid., 111.
[13] Ibid., 112.
[14] Ibid., 121.
[15] Ibid., 124.
[16] Ibid., 114.

[17] *Letters and Papers*, 93, 122.

[18] Bonhoeffer, 'Christmas Eve, 1943', *Letters and Papers from Prison* (1953), 61.

[19] Bonhoeffer, *Letters and Papers from Prison*, enlarged ed. (1971), 17.

[20] Bonhoeffer, 'April 30, 1944', *Letters and Papers from Prison* (1953), 92.

[21] Bonhoeffer, *Letters and Papers from Prison* (1953), 125.

[22] Bonhoeffer, *Letters and Papers from Prison* (1953), 99-100 with insertions from *Letters and Papers from Prison*, enlarged edition (1971), 302-3.

[23] Bonhoeffer, *Letters and Papers from Prison* (1953), 101.

[24] Jeff Keuss' blog 'U2 and Bonhoeffer's *cantus firmus*: Why we need music in our theology' (accessed March 25, 2012) http://www.jeffkeuss.com/blog/?p=1223.

[25] Jeremy Begbie, *Resounding Truth: Christian Wisdom in the World of Music*, (Grand Rapids: Baker Academic, 2007), 156-162.

[26] Bonhoeffer, 'December 18, 1943', *Letters and Papers from Prison* (1953)

[27] Bonhoeffer, *Letters and Papers from Prison* (1953), 57-58.

[28] Bonhoeffer, *Letters and Papers from Prison* (1953), 56-58.

[29] Scott Holland, 'First We Take Manhattan, Then We Take Berlin: Bonhoeffer's New York', *Cross Currents*, 50, no. 3 (2000).

Chapter 5: The New Atheists and the New Testament

Robert Martin

'The gospels are ancient fiction'[1] is the claim of the New Atheists. This modern, popular and militant group reject any sense of historical accuracy or reliability in the Gospels. The Bible is 'brimming with lies',[2] the Gospels are 'most certainly not literal truth',[3] are not 'reliable accounts of what happened in the real world',[4] and, 'cannot be introduced into a serious investigation'.[5] This conclusion is in harmony with the New Atheist assertion that religion is irrational—Christianity is belief without evidence.

If the Gospels *were* demonstrated as historically reliable the New Atheists would face two serious difficulties. The first concerns the miracles recorded there. The occurrence of miracles is inconsistent with a naturalistic world-view because their very definition requires a supernatural event to transcend ordinary happenings.[6]

The second difficulty concerns the claims of divinity Jesus makes. For example in Mark 2:1-12 Jesus claims to have authority to forgive sins, something that only God alone has prerogative to do. C. S. Lewis recognised the significance of his claims and wrote, 'In the mouth of any speaker who is not God, these words would imply what I can only regard as a silliness and conceit unrivalled by any other character in history'. Lewis concluded that 'a man who was merely a man and said the sort of things Jesus said would not be a great moral teacher. He would either be a lunatic—on a level with the man who says he is a poached egg—or else he would be the Devil of Hell.'[7] C. S. Lewis recognised that Jesus claimed to be divine.

If accurately recorded, the miracles and Jesus' divine self-understanding reported in the canonical Gospels would provide some *evidence* to believe in theism and the truth of Christianity. This in turn would seriously undermine the New Atheist assertion that religion is fundamentally irrational. Yet the truthfulness of the miracles recorded and Jesus' claims both rest on the premise that the Gospels are historical reliable—that what the Gospels record is what actually occurred in history. If the events did occur the New Atheist case is seriously weakened—Christianity is not irrational. The New Atheists recognise the criticalness of this link and attack the historical reliability of the Gospels with venom.[8]

The New Atheists assemble seven arguments attacking the historical reliability of the canonical gospels.[9]

1. Internal contradictions within the canonical Gospels

This is the most convincing argument for many of the New Atheists. They point out differences between the gospel accounts where they are claiming to record the same historical event. The authors of the Gospels can't 'agree on anything of importance'.[10] They make the contradictions in the infancy narratives a priority.[11] They also outline other alleged contradictions, for example, the date of Jesus' crucifixion,[12] the Sermon on the Mount, the anointing of Jesus, the treachery of Judas, Peter's 'denial', and the resurrection.[13] Hitchens claims these contradictions have never been explained except by the terms 'metaphor' or 'Christ of faith'.[14] These internal inconsistencies confirm two things to the New Atheists; first, the Gospels are unreliable as an historical record. Dawkins chides 'unsophisticated' Christians who think the Bible a literal and accurate record and hence 'evidence supporting their religious beliefs' by asking, '[W]hy don't they ever notice those glaring contradictions?'[15] Hitchens throws his hands up in the face of these differences: 'If the apostles do not know or cannot agree, of what use is my analysis'.[16] Secondly these inconsistencies confirm to the New Atheists that the Gospels do not have any 'divine' origin or authority. These contradictions provide incontrovertible evidence to Hitchens that religion is man-made.[17] Commenting on William Burr's *Self-Contradictions of the Bible*,[18] Harris neatly summarises the New Atheist position on Gospel internal inconsistencies: '[t]here is, perhaps, *no greater evidence* for the imperfection of the Bible as an account of reality, divine or mundane, than such instances of self-refutation.[19]

2. Denying the historical existence of Jesus

Hitchens[20] was the most adamant in this: '[C. S.] Lewis assumes on no firm evidence whatever that Jesus actually *was* a "character in history"'[21] and there was 'little or no evidence for the life of Jesus'.[22] Dennett and Dawkins both entertain this suggestion,[23] but conclude differently to Hitchens: Dawkins believes 'Jesus probably existed';[24] and Dennett also believes there was an historical Jesus of Nazareth.[25] Harris appears to accept the historical existence of Jesus, but as he casts much of the Bible as myth—the most comprehensive evidence for Jesus' existence—his precise position is unclear. If there were no historical figure of Jesus, Hitchens would be correct in suggesting the New Testament is historically unreliable, as it clearly assumes the existence of such a figure.

3. External contradictions with known history

The census recorded under Quirinius in Luke 2:1-3 is the most popular example of this.[26] Schürer summarises the five historical difficulties associated with Luke's census, which the New Atheists highlight: (First) history knows nothing of a general imperial census in Augustus' time; (Second) A Roman census would not have required Mary and Joseph to travel to Bethlehem; (Third) a Roman census would not have been made in Palestine during the time of King Herod; (Fourth) Josephus knows nothing of such a census and speaks of the census of AD 7 as something new; (Fifth) Quirinius was never governor of Syria during the lifetime of Herod.[27] Stenger adds further external contradictions via the silence of corroborating external evidence for the slaughter of the innocents (Matt 2:16) and the extraordinary events recorded in Matt 27:51-54.[28]

5. Unreliable transmission of the Gospel tradition

The New Atheists identify two areas of unreliable transmission. The first is the unreliable oral history of the Gospel tradition. They liken this to 'Chinese whispers'[29] involving 'hearsay upon hearsay'.[30] To Hitchens this helps explain the contradictions between Gospels.[31] Uniquely amongst the New Atheists, Stenger recognises the role eye-witness testimony plays in the oral tradition of the Gospel accounts yet dismisses it as being 'notoriously unreliable'.[32] The second is unreliable textual transmission. They claim the Gospels, once written, were 'recopied through fallible scribes'.[33] Harris suggests the texts have not retained their integrity over time.[34] Hitchens suggests the New Testament shows, 'unmistakable signs of having been tampered with'.[35] Furthermore the New Atheists also share a common interest in the work and story of Bart Ehrman.[36] They recommend or quote his *Misquoting Jesus*[37] and outline his journey from 'Bible-believing fundamentalist to thoughtful sceptic'[38] who 'could not reconcile his faith with his scholarship'.[39] Moreover they suggest that Ehrman has exposed the 'huge uncertainty befogging the New Testament texts'.[40] Perceived unreliable textual transmission is compounded by the suggestion that the documents were written long after the purported events.[41]

5. The Gospels were 'reverse-engineered' to conform to the Old Testament.

The most commonly cited example of this concerns the virgin birth and the 'prophecy' of Isaiah 7:14. Harris and Hitchens point out that the Greek *parthenos* (virgin) was a mistranslation of the original Hebrew *'almâ*, which simply meant 'young woman'.[42] They conclude the virgin birth was fabricated to make Jesus' birth conform to scripture.[43] Other examples are cited, notably the concern to place Jesus' birth in Bethlehem to fulfill Micah 5:2,[44] the Sermon on the Mount replicating Moses on Mount Sinai, and the disciples standing in for the Jews who followed Moses.[45] They conclude that the Gospels are unhistorical and fabricated; simply 'rehashed'[46] or 'reverse-engineered'[47] from the Old Testament.[48]

6. The Gnostic Gospels were equal competitors in describing the historical Jesus.

The New Atheists assert the canonical Gospels were chosen arbitrarily from a wider selection of competitors.[49] Hitchens asserted that these Gnostic Gospels were 'of the same period and provenance as many of the subsequently canonical and "authorised" Gospels'.[50] Whilst agreeing the

Gnostic Gospels had equal claim to canonisation, they disagree on the status of the Gnostic Gospels. Hitchens suggests that the Gnostic Gospels were 'fractionally more credible than the official account'[51] whereas Dawkins suggest those omitted were 'even more embarrassingly implausible' than the canonical ones.[52]

7. The ancient people were naive and ignorant

Here the New Atheist contempt for the ancients reaches its zenith. Harris suggests that '[t]he Bible, it seems certain, was the work of sand-strewn men and women who thought the earth was flat and for whom a wheelbarrow would have been a breathtaking example of emerging technology'.[53] Hitchens concurs, 'Religion comes from a period of human prehistory where nobody ... had the smallest idea of what was going on'.[54] Not only were the ancients ignorant, they were gullible, possessing no critical faculties. They propose that the Gospels were only persuasive to people not used to asking critical questions,[55] and were written in a milieu where low standards of evidence prevailed.[56] Harris sees further evidence of this in the 'poor scholarship' of the Gospels—citing Matthew's attribution of a prophecy to Jeremiah (Mt 27:9-10), when it appears in Zechariah.[57]

These factors all contribute to the conclusion that the canonical Gospels are historically unreliable. The New Atheists conclude that virtually no accurate history of any kind is recorded in the Gospels. The Gospels occupy the status of 'legends' and are 'not an honest attempt at history'.[58] Hitchens categorically states that the Gospels are 'most certainly not literal truth'.[59] Therefore, to the New Atheists, the legendary status of the Gospels renders Jesus' claims to divinity void (if he even existed at all) and the miracles invalid. Christianity is indeed irrational.

Responding to these claims

These appear formidable arguments to the historical trustworthiness of the canonical Gospels. Yet, the force of their objections is reduced upon closer scrutiny and reflection. The New Atheist conclusions regarding the historical reliability of the Gospels are neither satisfactory nor convincing. They make a number of methodological mistakes when assessing the historical witness to Jesus and they fail to adequately account for all of the evidence.

1. They make many assertions without evidence

The New Atheists make numerous assertions without appropriate evidence to support their claim. The most glaring instance of this is by *denying the historical existence of Jesus*. Hitchens presents no evidence to support his assertion of Jesus' non-existence.[60] He fails to account for the emergence of the New Testament writings and the references to Jesus in hostile material (i.e. references in Suetonius, Tacitus and Josephus). Compounding this, most historians do accept his existence. The most popular *Jesus myth* author, G.A. Wells,[61] mentioned by Dawkins, is not even an historian! Wells is one of the few modern scholars to argue Jesus never existed.[62] Yet in a more recent work even he admitted an 'itinerant Galilean preacher' existed.[63] The claim that Jesus never existed is made without evidence.

Similar assertions without evidence are made concerning the *importance and provenance of the Gnostic Gospels*. Dawkins asserts the Gospels chosen were chosen 'more or less arbitrarily'[64] without any discussion or evidence supporting his claim. Contrary to Dawkins' position it is generally accepted that many of the Gnostic Gospels were *not* of the same period and provenance as the canonical Gospels.[65] Debate instead centres around a subset of these 'Gospels'.[66] Further, since these 'Gospels' demonstrate awareness of late streams of canonical Gospel tradition, they are very likely to be dated later than the canonical Gospels.[67]

Finally, they provide no evidence to support their assertion that *the ancient people were naive and ignorant*.

It is ironic that for a group which trumpets the importance of evidence-based reasoning that a number of their claims are made without evidence or reasoning. This seriously weakens their arguments and credibility especially where the evidence contradicts their claims.

2. The New Atheists largely ignore important counter evidence.

Many of the assertions made by the New Atheists often ignore crucial counterevidence. The most glaring example of this is in their discussion of the *gospel transmission process* approximating it to Chinese whispers. Their analysis ignores serious, scholarly discussions which present formidable arguments against their position. Contrary to New Atheist assertions the textual transmission history of the New Testament is outstanding. F. F. Bruce applies the same criteria for determining the reliability of other ancient documents to the New Testament.[68] He highlights the overwhelming numbers of extant manuscripts and their closeness, relative to other ancient historical documents, to the time of the events they purport, to record a powerful argument for the manuscript fidelity of the New Testament.[69] Bruce notes, 'There is no body of ancient literature in the world which enjoys such a wealth of good textual attestation as the New Testament.'[70] He concludes, 'If the New Testament were a collection of secular writings, their authenticity would generally be regarded as beyond all doubt'.[71] Yet the New Atheists ignore this.

Similar ignorance is evident in discussion of *Gospel genre*. They claim the Gospels are 'not an honest attempt at history'.[72] Yet this overlooks Luke's prologue (Luke 1:1-4) where he outlines his authorial method, which is fundamentally historical—Luke consults eyewitnesses and carefully investigates everything from the beginning. Furthermore, the New Atheist claim also ignores the broad affinities the Gospels display to the Greco-Roman biographies (*bioi*). Both *bioi* and the Gospels present continuous prose narratives comprising stories, anecdotes, sayings and speeches focused on the main character.[73] Understanding Gospel genre this way affords an important hermeneutical bridge; the Gospels do offer a degree of interpretation about their subjects, but importantly they are also treated historically like any other ancient biography as they had to maintain a 'recognizable continuity with the historical person'.[74] The Gospels do purport to record history and this evidence is ignored by the New Atheists.

3. The New Atheists fail to understand the logic of fulfilment

The New Atheists suggest Matthew fabricated events, such as the virgin birth or the slaughter of the innocents, in order to conform to Old Testament prophecies. However this represents a failure to understand Matthew's logic. The very point of *fulfilment* requires there to be *something* which corresponds to the scriptural pattern. It appears more likely the Old Testament quotation was associated with an already existing tradition. Richard France rightly concludes, 'Matthew is not simply meditating on Old Testament texts, but claiming that in what has happened they find a fulfillment. If the events are legendary, the argument is futile.'[75]

4. Their methodology precludes them from making the wide reaching conclusions they assert

The New Atheist method of ascertaining historical trustworthiness of the Gospels involves selecting a few examples of disagreement or difficulty and then extrapolating to the whole and concluding the *entire* document unreliable. A good example is with the external contradictions with known history and Luke's census; the New Atheists notice the difficulties of reconciling Luke's account with known history and therefore conclude the entire document historically unreliable.

Yet this methodology breaks down when at other points in his narrative *Luke is consistent with known history*. Luke's dating of the beginning of John the Baptists ministry in Luke 3:1 cannot be challenged for accuracy—he even identifies the obscure Lysanias of Abielene.[76] Luke is consistently accurate with geographic details, and a number of the practices recorded in the Gospels have been confirmed by archaeological evidence. Onfray suggested that crucified persons were never buried in tombs. Yet this assertion fails to reconcile with an archaeological discovery made in 1968. On the outskirts of Jerusalem a Jewish tomb dating to the first century was unearthed. In the tomb were the skeletal remains of a man who had been crucified—an iron nail had been found pierced through the man's foot.

After spending much time investigating the archaeological integrity of Luke, the famed archaeologist Sir William Ramsay eventually concluded that 'Luke is a historian of the first rank; not merely are his statements of fact trustworthy ... [he] should be placed along with the very greatest of historians'.[77]

Much of the Gospels are historically reliable and consistent with our knowledge of the ancient world and this becomes problematic for the New Atheists when they declare the Gospels 'legends'. It is simply unfair to the Gospel writers to accuse them of complete historical unreliability. The many agreements with our understanding of ancient history render the New Atheist conclusions of complete historical unreliability premature.

5. The New Atheists misunderstand ancient historiography: Contradictions often occur between ancient historical documents.

The New Atheists make much mileage by the perceived contradictions in the Gospels. The New Atheists give the impression that the Gospel writers fail to agree on 'anything of importance',[78] and that there are 'glaring contradictions'[79] in their accounts. Their conclusion is that the documents are historically unreliable. Yet they overstate their case and they misunderstand ancient historiography: Contradictions occur between ancient historical documents which don't automatically render these documents historically unreliable.

It is first worthwhile clarifying the two different types of 'contradiction'. The first is a *contradiction of fact*. This is where one historian records a fact, number, or event where another historian offers an irreconcilable alternative. For example, a contradiction of fact exists between Josephus and Tacitus in recording the number of people besieged in the Jewish War; Josephus records 6,000 whereas Tacitus records 600,000.[80] There is no way of reconciling these divergent numbers. Unless we have misunderstood the historian's intention, one or the other (or both) is wrong. Repeatedly occurring contradictions of fact in parallel accounts raises questions pertaining to the historical reliability of one or both of the accounts.

The second type of contradiction is a *contradiction of silence*. One historian records an event or detail another historian fails to record.

Contradictions of silence occur for several reasons; (First) the historians utilise different sources, hence certain facts available to one are unavailable to the other; (Second) the historian deliberately supplements material already known to the readers from another source; hence one account will be silent; (Third) the historians have manipulated the historical data differently. There are numerous ways this can lead to contradictions of silence: the historians may have different agendas, and hence emphasise and record certain events in greater detail and omit other details they deem less important to their purpose; economy of presentation may lead historians to omit historical details unnecessary to their purpose; and the practice of paraphrase was a common feature of ancient histories where the *ipsissima vox* (actual voice) rather than the *ipsissima verba* (actual words) was utilised leading to variations and differences between accounts.[81] Moreover, the oral history of an historical tradition may leave variations.

A contradiction of silence may indicate a contradiction of fact, but not necessarily. Most importantly, silence does not strictly constitute a contradiction. In many cases reconciliation of the two accounts is possible: both accounts may be historically accurate even when recounting different details. Thus care must be taken before declaring contradictions of silence historically inaccurate.

Contradictions of silence and fact occur regularly in ancient history. Two historians, Polybius and Titus Livius (Livy) recount Hannibal crossing the Alps and there are contradictions between their accounts.

Notable contradictions of fact include the route Hannibal took across the Alps.[82] Polybius records Hannibal's army seeing Italy (the plain of Po) from the summit of the Alps *before* descending but Livy records them

sighting the plain of Po *after* the army had begun to advance.[83] Both
authors also disagree on the number of troops Hannibal took across the
Alps. Polybius records 12,000 African and 8,000 Iberian foot soldiers and
not more than 6,000 horse[84] whereas Livy, acknowledging other
estimates—even citing Polybius' figures—ultimately suggests Hannibal
brought 80,000 foot and 10,000 horse into Italy.[85]

Contradictions of silence also exist between the accounts. Only Livy
records the method of cutting through the rocks on their descent. He
describes how the soldiers cut down trees, setting fire to the timber and
heating the rock, which after application of vinegar rendered the rocks
soft and crumbling.[86] Polybius knows nothing of fire and vinegar, simply
suggesting the soldiers set to work to 'build up the path along the cliff, a
most toilsome task'.[87] Only Polybius records the olive-branches and
wreaths used by certain barbarians as gestures of friendship towards
Hannibal,[88] yet Livy records only a verbal encounter.[89] These
contradictions of silence are clearly reconcilable. In fact, at many points
in the narrative Livy provides more detail than Polybius, perhaps
indicating he uses Polybius as a source and deliberately supplements his
material with additional material.[90]

The contradictions of silence between Livy and Polybius generally only
occur regarding circumstantial details.[91] Yet glaring contradictions of
silence concerning whole events exist between Josephus and Philo in their
accounts of Gaius' attack on the Jewish Temple in AD 40.[92] Philo alone
records a prelude to the episode; how Jews earlier pulled down a statue
erected to Gaius' honour in Jamnia.[93] Philo alone also recounts the
Roman legate's (Publius Petronius) actions immediately following Gaius'
decree; summoning Jewish leaders to explain and accept Gaius' intentions
and hence prevent opposition to this provocative act.[94] Josephus is silent
regarding both events. Furthermore, both historians agree Agrippa
successfully intervened with Gaius to save the temple, but disagree over
his methods of tackling the problem. Philo suggests that after a serious
illness Agrippa wrote Gaius a long letter which Gaius heeded.[95] However
Josephus writes nothing concerning any illness and suggests that Agrippa

invited Gaius to a sumptuous banquet where Gaius granted Agrippa's request.[96]

These contradictions of silence can be reconciled, the events recorded by both historians may have actually occurred. Mary Smallwood, whilst generally regarding Philo as more reliable than Josephus, concedes that 'the literary picture of Gaius given by Suetonius ... suggests that a banquet would have been more to Gaius' taste than a twenty-five-hundred word memorandum'.[97] She goes on to suggest that it was 'not impossible to combine the two versions and suppose that Agrippa attempted to soften Gaius up with a banquet before presenting him with the cold facts in writing'.[98] Thus these contradictions of silence can conceivably be reconciled -fabrication should not be the automatic supposition explaining such 'contradictions'.

These 'contradictions' also likely indicate that Philo and Josephus wrote independently.[99]

Contradictions are also evident even in historical events recorded by the same author—Josephus contradicts himself. In his autobiography *Life of Josephus,* Josephus rescued Tiberias from being sacked by the Galileans,[100] yet in his *Jewish War* he delivered it over to his soldiers to plunder.[101] Contradictions like these threaten the credibility of Josephus as an historian—and some do challenge his credibility.[102] However, a number of recent archaeological discoveries have vindicated many of Josephus' descriptions causing some to hold a higher view of Josephus' historical trustworthiness. Per Bilde closes his discussion on the historical reliability of Josephus vindicating the historian: '[t]herefore we must come to the conclusion, that, to a high degree, Josephus' personal engagement and his personal interpretation of the historical material appears to be offset by a passionate historical interest in what actually took place'.[103]

In assessing these contradictions, no modern historian suggests the described events never took place, i.e. that Hannibal never crossed the Alps or that Gaius never attacked the Jewish Temple. Neither do historians suggest that historical information cannot be gleaned from the alternative history. Instead, careful reconstruction of the past is made through rigorous analysis of the alternative sources. Yet, if the conclusions of the New Atheists regarding the Gospel contradictions are applied to these other ancient histories, then these documents should also be rejected as unreliable. Subsequently, this would result in the questioning of much ancient history severely diminishing our knowledge of the ancient world. It is far too simplistic to suggest that differences in the Gospel accounts immediately render them historically unreliable; such a conclusion fails to consider the nature of ancient historiography. Contradictions occur regularly in ancient historiography and fabrication and unreliability should not be the automatic supposition explaining such contradictions.

6. The new atheists overstate their case: there are important agreements between the Gospels

The New Atheists overstate the nature and extent of *contradictions* in the New Testament. Most of the contradictions cited by the New Atheists are contradictions of silence where reconciliation *is* possible. For example, both Jesus and Simon could have carried Jesus' cross, where Jesus initially began the task but was too weak to continue and hence Simon finished the job. The Gospel authors may offer different perspectives because they were dependent on different sources or were intent on emphasising a certain historical reality in order to make a theological point.

Furthermore, the New Atheists overlook important *agreements* between the Gospels. They train their sights on the infancy narratives and claim that the differences between Matthew and Luke's accounts are 'glaring'.[104] Yet this is a misleading conclusion for Matthew and Luke agree on many core facts of the narratives. They both agree that the 'parents' of Jesus were Mary and Joseph.[105] They both agree that Mary was pledged/betrothed to Joseph and before they came together Mary was found to be with child from the Holy Spirit.[106] They agree that Jesus was born in Bethlehem in the line of David at the time of King Herod () and that he grew up in Nazareth.[107] Both also correctly identify the relevant geographic districts: Nazareth is in Galilee and Bethlehem in Judea.[108]

There are many similarities between the presentations of Jesus' birth and there are no contradictions of fact concerning these core elements. Instead through the criterion of 'multiple attestation' these agreements actually strengthen the case for the historical reliability of the core of the infancy narratives. [109]

The New Atheist claims have great rhetorical power, yet are misleading. Many of the contradictions they claim are contradictions of silence and there is significant agreement between the key features of the two infancy narratives. Again, their conclusions fail to adequately account for all the evidence.

Conclusion

The New Atheists claim too much. They fail to support their, often wild, assertions with rigorous well-reasoned evidence. They misunderstand ancient historiography and the nature of historical reporting. They overlook important agreements in the infancy narratives and the contradictions they cite do not render the Gospels unreliable historical documents.

Consistent contradictions of fact would render documents historically unreliable, yet most of the contradictions cited by the New Atheists are contradictions of silence where plausible solutions exist to explain the differences. These contradictions often arise as the Gospel authors manipulate their historical sources differently. Craig Blomberg's conclusion is apt: 'Most of these proposals readily concede that the evangelists freely reworded and rearranged the traditions they inherited, but not to the extent that their Gospels should be considered historically unreliable'.[110]

The New Atheist conclusions may easily evade the theistic implications present in the claims and deeds of the Jesus of the Gospels. But such conclusions are not reached on rigorous evidence-based reasoning. Their conclusions fail to adequately account for the evidence. It is ironic that a group so intent on rationality and evidence can overlook and ignore so much. The New Atheist case against the reliability of the canonical Gospels is hardly proven.

---

[1] Richard Dawkins, *The God Delusion*, (London: Bantam, 2006), 97.

[2] Sam Harris, *Letter to a Christian Nation*, (New York: Alfred A. Knopf, 2006), 49.

[3] Christopher Hitchens, *God Is Not Great*, (New York: Twelve, 2007), 120.

[4] Dawkins, *The God Delusion*, 92-93, see also 97.

[5] Daniel Dennett, *Breaking the Spell*, (London: Allen Lane, 2006), 240.

[6] B.L. Blackburn, 'Miracles and Miracle Stories' in *Dictionary of Jesus and The Gospels*, ed. Joel B. Green and Scot McKnight (Downers Grove: Intervarsity Press, 1992), 549.

[7] C.S. Lewis, *Mere Christianity*, (London: Fontana, 1952), 52-53.

[8] See also Victor Stenger, *God: The Failed Hypothesis*, (Amherst, N.Y.: Prometheus Books, 2007), 188., and NAME Onfray, *The Atheist Manifesto*, (Melbourne: Melbourne University Press, 2005), 117.

[9] Dennett never comprehensively outlines his position on the historical reliability of the Gospels; though he does describe the Bible as, '*presumed* historical documentation'. Dennett, *Breaking the Spell*, 240. Emphasis mine.

[10] Hitchens, *God Is Not Great*, 111.

[11] Sam Harris, *The End of Faith*, (New York: W.W. Norton & Co., 2004), 95; Hitchens, *God Is Not Great*, 111; Dawkins, *The God Delusion*, 93-95.

[12] Harris, *Letter to a Christian Nation*, 58-59.

[13] Hitchens, *God Is Not Great*, 112; Stenger, *God: The Failed Hypothesis*, 180, highlights the inconsistency in the resurrection accounts.

[14] Hitchens, *God Is Not Great*, 115. Consistent with David Strauss who suggested once the mythical view of scriptural interpretation (consonant with Christ of faith) was admitted, 'the innumerable, and never otherwise to be harmonised, discrepancies and chronological contradictions in the gospel histories disappear, as it were, at one stroke'. David Friedrich Strauss, *The Life of Jesus Critically Examined*, (Philadelphia: SCM Press, 1973), 57.

[15] Dawkins, *The God Delusion*, 94.

[16] Hitchens, *God Is Not Great*, 115.

[17] Ibid.

[18] William H. Burr, *Self Contradictions of the Bible,* (Buffalo, N.Y.: Prometheus Books, 1987, Originally published *Self Contradictions of the Bible* (New York: A.J. Davis, 1860).

[19] Harris, *The End of Faith,* 244; Harris, *Letter to a Christian Nation,* 58. Emphasis mine.

[20] Onfray also denies the historical existence of Jesus (Onfray, *The Atheist Manifesto,* 117).

[21] Hitchens, *God Is Not Great,* 119. Italics original.

[22] Ibid., 127. Hitchens concedes the evangelists' efforts to 'massage' the evidence to fulfill prophecies may be 'inverse proof' that 'someone of later significance *was* born' (Hitchens, *God Is Not Great,* 114), but dismisses this due to the contradictions within the Gospels.

[23] Dawkins, *The God Delusion,* 97; Dennett's Sherlock Holmes allegory (*Breaking the Spell,* 212-213), was intended to raise the possibility (confirmed by personal email (March 10, 2009).

[24] Dawkins, *The God Delusion,* 97.

[25] Dennett, personal email (March 10, 2009).

[26] Dawkins, *The God Delusion,* 93-94; Hitchens, *God Is Not Great,* 112; Stenger, *God: The Failed Hypothesis,* 178.

[27] Emil Schürer, *A History of the Jewish People in the Time of Jesus Christ, Volume 2* (Edinburgh: T&T Clark, 1892), 114-143.

[28] Stenger, *God: The Failed Hypothesis,* 178-179.

[29] Dawkins, *The God Delusion,* 93.

[30] Hitchens, *God Is Not Great,* 120.

[31] Ibid.

[32] Stenger, *God: The Failed Hypothesis,* 179.

[33] Dawkins, *The God Delusion,* 93.

[34] Harris, *The End of Faith,* 20; Harris, *The Moral Landscape: How Science Can Determine Human Values,* (New York: Free Press, 2010), footnote 82, 252.

[35] Hitchens, *God Is Not Great,* 110.

[36] Bart Ehrman, *Misquoting Jesus: The Story of Who Changed the Bible and Why,* (San Francisco: Harper San Francisco, 2005)

[37] Dawkins, *The God Delusion,* 95; Hitchens, *God Is Not Great,* 120-122; Harris, *Letter to a Christian Nation,* 92.

[38] Dawkins, *The God Delusion,* 95.

[39] Hitchens, *God Is Not Great*, 120.

[40] Dawkins, *The God Delusion*, 95.

[41] Hitchens, *God Is Not Great*, 110,111,143; Dawkins, *The God Delusion*, 93; Harris, *The Moral Landscape*, footnote 82, 252.

[42] Harris, *The End of Faith*, 94-95; Harris, *Letter to a Christian Nation*, 58; Hitchens, *God Is Not Great*, 115.

[43] Harris, *The End of Faith*, 95.

[44] Dawkins, *The God Delusion*, 93; Hitchens, *God Is Not Great*, 114.

[45] Hitchens, *God Is Not Great*, 115-6.

[46] Dawkins, *The God Delusion*, 96.

[47] Hitchens, *God Is Not Great*, 116.

[48] See also, Stenger, *God: The Failed Hypothesis*, 179.

[49] Dawkins, *The God Delusion*, 95; Hitchens, *God Is Not Great*, 112-3; Dennett, *Breaking the Spell*, 145, 167.

[50] Hitchens, *God Is Not Great*, 112.

[51] Ibid. 113.

[52] Dawkins, *The God Delusion*, 96.

[53] Harris, *The End of Faith*, 45.

[54] Hitchens, *God Is Not Great*, 64.

[55] Dawkins, *The God Delusion*, 92.

[56] Harris, *The End of Faith*, 77.

[57] Harris, *Letter to a Christian Nation*, 58.

[58] Dawkins, *The God Delusion*, 96.

[59] Hitchens, *God Is Not Great*, 120.

[60] Onfray, to his credit, does attempt counter-explanations for the non-biblical evidence often marshalled for Jesus' existence. He proposes the ancient histories by Josephus, Suetonius, and Tacitus embellished by anonymous monks (Onfray, *The Atheist Manifesto*, 117). However Onfray's proposals are unconvincing; why would Christians interpolate Tacitus and describe their faith as a deadly 'superstition' that fosters 'shameful' acts? (For more details see: Paul R. Eddy and Gregory A. Boyd, *The Jesus Legend: A Case for the Historical Reliability of the Synoptic Tradition*, (Grand Rapids: Baker Academic, 2007), 172-199, part. 176-177 (Suetonius), 180-181 (Tacitus), 190-198 (Josephus).

[61] Who wrote 'Did Jesus Exist?' mentioned by Dawkins (Dawkins, *The God Delusion*, 97.).

[62] John Dickson, *The Christ Files: How Historians Know What They Know About Jesus*, (Sydney: Blue Bottle Books, 2006), 9.

[63] G.A. Wells, *The Jesus Myth*, (Chicago: Open Court, 1999), 103.

[64] Dawkins, *The God Delusion*, 95.

[65] The Gospel of Philip, the Gospel of Truth, the Proto-Gospel of James, and the Infancy Gospel of Thomas date from the second century, Helmut Koester, *Ancient Christian Gospels: Their History and Development*, (London: SCM Press, 1990), 22,23,309.

[66] The Gospel of Thomas, The Gospel of Peter, and Papyrus Egerton 2. See Craig A. Evans, 'Gospels, Extra-New Testament' in *Encyclopedia of the Historical Jesus*, ed. Craig A. Evans, (New York: Routledge, 2008): 261-263.

[67] Ibid.

[68] F. F. Bruce, *The New Testament Documents: Are They Reliable?*, 8th ed.; (London: IVF, 1960), 5.

[69] Ibid., 14-16.

[70] F. F. Bruce, *The Books and the Parchments: Some Chapters on the Transmission of the Bible*, 2nd ed., (London: Pickering & Inglis, 1953), 170.

[71] Bruce, *The New Testament Documents: Are They Reliable?*, 15.

[72] Dawkins, *The God Delusion*, 96.

[73] See Richard A. Burridge, *What are the Gospels? A Comparison with Graeco-Roman Biography*, 2nd ed., (Grand Rapids: Eerdmans, 2004); Richard A. Burridge, 'Gospel as Genre', Pages 232-236 in *Encyclopedia of the Historical Jesus*, ed. Craig A. Evans (New York: Routledge, 2008) 232-236.

[74] Burridge, 'Gospel as Genre', 234.

[75] Richard T. France, 'Herod and the Children of Bethlehem' *Novum Testamentum*, 21 (1979): 120.

[76] A. N. Sherwin-White, Roman Society and Roman Law in the *New Testament: The Sarum Lectures 1960-1961*, (Grand Rapids, Mi.: Baker, 1963), 166-167.

[77] Sir William Ramsay, *The Bearing of Recent Discoveries on the Trustworthiness of the New Testament*, (London: Hodder & Stoughton, 1915) 222.

[78] Hitchens, *God Is Not Great*, 111.

[79] Dawkins, *The God Delusion*, 94.

[80] Josephus, *Jewish War* 6.284: Tacitus, *Histories* 5.13.

[81] Craig L. Blomberg, *The Historical Reliability of the Gospels*, 2nd ed., (Downers Grove: Intervarsity, 2007), 157.

[82] Gibbon suggests 'Livy carries Hannibal over the Cottian Alps, properly Mount Genevre ... Polybius leads him by the Summus Pennius, or Great St. Bernard', Edward Gibbon, *The Miscellaneous Works of Edward Gibbon Esq*, (London: B. Blake, 1837), 501. Proctor has more recently proposed no conflict between the routes—once Livy's mistakes have been corrected. See Dennis Proctor, *Hannibal's March in History*, (Oxford: Clarendon Press, 1971), 179-184.

[83] Polybius, 3.54; Livy, 21.35.

[84] Polybius, 56.4

[85] Livy, 21.38

[86] Livy, 21.37

[87] Polybius, 3.55.6

[88] Polybius, 3.52.3

[89] Livy, 21.34

[90] See, John.F. Lazenby, *Hannibal's War: A Military History of the Second Punic War*, (Warminster: Aris & Phillips, 1978), 260. Alternatively both could have used a common source. See Serge Lancel, *Hannibal*, (Tr. Antonia Nevill; Oxford: Blackwell, 1998), 27.

[91] To borrow a term from Murray Harris, *Raised Immortal: Resurrection and Immortality in the New Testament*, (Grand Rapids, Mich.: Eerdmans, 1985), 68.

[92] See, E. Mary Smallwood, 'Philo and Josephus as Historians of the Same Events', in *Josephus, Judaism, and Christianity* ed. Louis H. Feldman and Gohei Hata (Leiden: Brill, 1987), 114-132. Particularly pages 120-125.

[93] Philo, *On the Embassy to Gaius* 200-203

[94] *On the Embassy to Gaius* 221-224

[95] *On the Embassy to Gaius* 261-331

[96] Josephus, *Jewish Antiquities* 18.289-301

[97] Smallwood, 'Philo & Josephus as Historians of the Same Events', 124.

[98] Ibid.

[99] Recognised by Smallwood, Ibid., 124-125.

[100] Josephus, *Life of Josephus* 381-389

[101] *Jewish War* 2.646; Uriel Rappaport, 'Where was Josphus Lying—In His *Life* or in the *War*?', in *Josephus & the History of the Greco-Roman Period: Essays in*

Memory of Morton Smith, ed. Fausto Parente & Joseph Sievers, (Leiden: Brill, 1994), 282-283.

[102] For example Louis H. Feldman, 'Flavius Josephus Revisited: The Man, His Writings, and His Significance,' in *Aufstieg und Niedergang Der Römischen Welt. Geschichte und Kulter Roms im Spiegel der neueren Forschung* ed. H. Temporini and W. Haase (Berlin: de Gruyter, 1984), 862.

[103] Per Bilde, *Flavius Josephus between Jerusalem and Rome: His Life, his Works, and their Importance*, (Sheffield: JSOT, 1988), 199-200.

[104] Dawkins, *The God Delusion*, 94.

[105] Matt 1:16; Luke 1:27, 2:4-5

[106] Matt 1:18; Luke 1:27; Matt 1:18; Luke 1:34-35

[107] Matt 2:1; Luke 2:4-7; Matt 1:20; Luke 2:4; Matt 2:1; Luke 2:4-7; Matt 1:22-23; Luke 2:39

[108] Matt 2:1, 2:22-23; Luke 2:4

[109] John P. Meier, *A Marginal Jew: Rethinking the Historical Jesus, Volume One: The Roots of the Problem and the Person*, (New York: Doubleday, 1991), 213-214.

[110] Blomberg, *The Historical Reliability of the Gospels*, 195.

Chapter 6: Can We Be Good Without God?

Justin Denholm

We hear many voices in our society talking about how we should live. Amongst them, there are people arguing that you can indeed be good without God. They say that God, or religious moral codes, provide one avenue for goodness. A belief in God might, for instance, lead us to care deeply about the environment and to work hard to protect it as God's creation. Equally, though, someone who is not religious may develop a real and genuine passion for caring for the physical world that sustains us. Both people, it is said, do good things in caring for the world, but from very different motivations.

Others dispute this, and suggest that we can indeed only be good with God. We sometimes see this reflected in public defence of the Christian moral standard, while on other occasions this position might arise from Islamic teaching. This argument holds that ethical teaching is from God, and is the only way to be good; therefore, we must fight to preserve these moral standards in our laws and public life. Some people walk this line because they believe that their moral code is the best standard for society to flourish regardless of personal faith, others because they feel that individuals and societies acting well create conditions where others are more likely to come to faith. Whatever the reasons, we hear these voices asserting that you cannot be good without God.

In recent years, another voice has been added to the public debate around this question. This voice is strident, and insists not only that people can be good without God, but in fact that we can *only* be good without God. This camp includes the authors arguing that religion 'poisons everything', and also many people simply watching the long procession of cases of sexual abuse at the hands of clergy. Whether or not this is the sole or foremost reason, I've had a number of sad conversations with people who tell me they walked away from the church over moral issues—a deeply practical expression that, to be good, one must be rid of God.

Are these the only options? Is there another voice? Before we can consider these conversations and how we might engage with them from a Christian perspective, we first need to resolve the confusion that exists around each of these ideas. We can do this best by thinking biblically about these questions. What is goodness, and how does it relate to God? How is morality defined and expressed? What relevance does this have to the real questions people are asking today?

From the outset, Christians believe that God is the creator of all things. He made the world and all that is in it, and when he finished his work he could look on it and say that it was very good (Gen 1:31). For the world to be good doesn't mean that it does nice things but that when it was made it was just as it should be. All creation was properly ordered, and in right relationship with God and itself. This proper pattern for existence is one aspect of what goodness means today. Goodness is seen when we think and act in the way we were intended to, when we are in right relationship with God and with his creation (Gen 1:26).

Goodness in the Bible is also about God's character and his nature. 'The Lord is good, and his love endures forever' (Ps 100:5). We are told of God's goodness, seen in his displays of mercy, generosity and truthfulness, all of which we are told are not simply things that God does, but reflections of his consistent character (e.g. Heb 6:18). John Calvin described God as the 'inexhaustible fountain of good', whose very nature made it impossible for anything other than good to emanate from him. God's goodness is not merely an intrinsic quality that defines who he is but a standard to which we are called in relationship. 'You shall be holy for I the Lord am holy' we read in Leviticus 19:2 (echoed too in 1 Peter 1:16).

We are also reminded that God is not just one of many who are good, but that there is no one good except God (Mt 19:17). In this passage, Jesus is asked a variant of the question we have before us: How can we be good? Jesus's reply is revealing. He does not offer an answer in terms of the actions a person should do but instead tells the young man where he should be looking: to God, the author and standard of goodness. In the encyclical *Veritatis Splendor*, John Paul II explains, 'Jesus shows that the young man's question is really a religious question, and that the goodness that attracts and at the same time obliges man has its source in God, and indeed is God himself. God alone is worthy of being loved "with all one's heart, and with all one's soul, and with all one's mind." (Mt 22:37)' God is both the source of goodness and the standard by which goodness is measured.

Clearly, when we consider goodness in these two ways, in terms of right relationships and God's character, we can see that it is inseparable from God within a Christian world-view. God is the creator of the world and the one who puts it in order. Moreover, the standard by which goodness comes is God's own nature. This is about the *ontologic* nature of goodness (an exploration of what the essence of goodness really is): God is good, and goodness comes from God alone.

There is another way to consider goodness, though, which is about our *experience* of goodness in this world. This leads us in a somewhat different direction. Romans 1:20, for instance, tells us that the 'invisible qualities' of God have been evident in creation for all time. Some have taken this idea to relate primarily to the ordering of the physical universe. For example, Albert Einstein gestured at this idea when he remarked that 'the eternal mystery of the world is its comprehensibility'.[1] Certainly the ordering of the physical universe can provide a lens through which to appreciate the existence of a creator God. However, the framework of the moral universe also provides such a window. Even as our society debates whether such a thing as universal morality exists, and what its content might be, we acknowledge that we share together an impulse to be good. As Romans 2 goes on to make plain, people who do not recognise God can still act in a way we would consider to be morally correct. Why? Because God has 'written the law on their hearts' (Rom 2:15); their consciences lead them toward His standard of the good. This doesn't mean that they can achieve God's standard without Him, but that they are aware of the moral order even before they are able to understand or articulate why they are convinced of it. We should not be surprised by people who profess not to know God acting in good ways; this too is a sign of God's work in the world, of the 'rain that falls on the just and unjust alike'. (Mt 5:45)

Human beings are aware of the categories of right and wrong, even where we might disagree with aspects of moral content. As created humanity we long to be good and in right relationship with God. Christians understand, though, that being created in God's image is not the end of the story. We are a created people, but also a fallen people, who have universally turned away from God and need restoration. In a fallen world our intuitive knowledge and access to understanding of moral truths is fractured; as fallen people we both reject the good and continually fail to properly grasp it. This is important because mere experience of the moral universe can never be sufficient to allow us to be properly good. Taking our fallenness seriously, we can see that we are compromised in our ability to appreciate and rightly perceive the proper goals and aims of our lives; alone, we do not even know what we do not know. This does not mean that we will never take pleasure in doing good things, that we will never see them have a positive impact on the world around us, or that we will never act in some way according to God's intentions; these things are good gifts from God's creation, and their complete fulfillment is part of our hope as we long for the world to come. It does mean, though, that our desires and aims are unreliable guides to how God would have us live, and that our satisfaction can never be its yardstick. Even those of us who do know God remain part of a fallen world, and have a damaged capacity to appreciate what is right and how we should live. We trust that God will guide us in growing toward being people after his own heart, while knowing that in this world we will never achieve the standard we long for.

A biblical survey affirms the overarching reality of morality: God is the standard from which goodness is derived and its ultimate judge. All human beings are made in God's image, and our universal experience of the world reinforces for us the biblical message that morality is an intrinsic characteristic of humanity. Those with and those without a relationship with God both have access to a moral world and a common understanding about right and wrong, at least in a general and fallen sense.

This brings us back to one of the ways that language around these matters can get confusing. Have I just said that we can be good without God or not? Some might take these observations to mean that you can be good without God, because a personal relationship with God is not a prerequisite for moral activity. I would say, though, that you cannot be good without God, first because it is impossible to be 'without God' due to our nature as created beings, and second because God is the reality of goodness, and it is towards His image that any impulse at goodness gestures towards, however imperfectly.

Although I can make some assertions about our ultimate inability to be good without God, I still find myself uncomfortable with this as a starting point. One point of discomfort is theological, the other apologetic. Although I don't believe that either of these issues automatically arises from a belief in God's intrinsic necessity for morality, I encounter them frequently enough that it is worth addressing them here.

My theological concern is that when I hear the question 'Can you be good without God?' all I can think is that it misses a big part of the problem. The real problem comes when you realise that any meaningful system of ethics is impossible to fulfill properly. Plenty of people have a vague sense that they are 'good people', but anyone who has thought more deeply about how to be good comes up against the problem that goodness requires perfection. Utilitarians need to be able to understand all possible consequences and predict outcomes to an impossible degree. Virtue ethics asks that we control our character without flaw, that we find a perfect moral standard to aspire to and follow it without a slip or stumble. Those who want to follow principles have an unchanging moral code that judges every action, thought and intention and invariably finds them wanting. Failure is not a result of a particular approach; it is an inevitable outcome of who we are. Everyone who takes being good seriously has to grapple with the problem that we are human, and we cannot meet the standards that goodness asks of us.

Here is where the rubber hits the road for Christian ethics, because we, too, will fall short of what goodness demands. Christianity does not offer a moral code that can be exchanged in place of other ethical systems; what we believe is not simply a better way or a system of actions that will allow individuals or society to achieve goodness where other approaches have failed. Rather, the unique contribution of the Christian message is assurance of forgiveness. What we have to offer is grace. The power of the gospel is to understand that we are weak, and we are fallen, and we fail; and yet, when we were still sinners, Christ died for us (Rom 5:7-8). We serve a God whose power is most revealed in our weakness, not in our strength; a God who is most glorified in our repentance, not our self-righteousness. While our common humanity means that we all have capacity to grasp towards what is good, it is only through the death and resurrection of Jesus Christ that we can actually be good, as we surrender our own efforts to live well, and accept God's forgiveness and reconciliation (Romans 4:5).

My second concern comes from an apologetic perspective, as we think about conversations and engagement with people who don't share our faith in Christ, who consider themselves to be 'without God'. I speak with many non-believers who would consider themselves to be 'good people'. Some of them embarrass me with their thoughtful and self-sacrificial actions and their generous spirits; attributes that I admire and wish came more naturally to me. I cannot step back from the truth of the need for God in moral life, but I have not often found it productive to open a conversation by telling people that their attempts to live well are pointless. How can we be faithful to what we know to be true in a way that attracts people to the gospel instead of driving them away?

Here, I take some inspiration from the Apostle Paul as he speaks with the Athenians (Acts 17:16-34). In a memorable episode, Paul describes a statue erected to 'The Unknown God'. First, he praises the Athenians for their religious devotion, before going on to explain who the true God is, and who their devotion is properly directed towards. He acknowledges their attempts to honour God, but then goes on to explain to them the real truth that underlies the situation. Note, too, that Paul doesn't attack the Athenians for the plethora of statutes to other gods, even though he was distressed by them. Instead, he chooses to start from a point where he can offer some affirmation; at least with the intention, if not the execution!

I think we can do this, too. In our conversations with non-believers, instead of looking for elements of their morality that are in conflict with our faith, why not look for ways in which we can affirm common intentions while pointing towards deeper truths? Let me take the example of environmentalism. The impulse to care for and preserve our world is a good and laudable thing, and in my corner of Melbourne it is a trait often co-existing with atheism. Instead of telling people that their environmentalism is meaningless, let's show them why it really is meaningful—because God is creator and Lord, and because of a resurrected Christ who is coming to redeem and recreate our world.

Ultimately, if what we mean by being good is about trying to live well, we should freely acknowledge that all people have this capacity. To our atheist friends, the question 'Can you be good without God?' runs the risk of making the arrogant suggestion that those of us who know God are already good, that the act of affiliating oneself with a church or a faith community makes a person morally superior. We are not good, and as much as we want to, we will never be good in our own strength. As we long to be right with God, let's not forget that when we come together as Christians it is not to celebrate how good we are. Instead, we come together to acknowledge our inability to be good, to confess our failures and to celebrate the forgiveness we have found in Christ.

---

1. Albert Einstein, 'Physics and Reality', *Journal of the Franklin Institute*, 221, no. 3 (1936): 349-382.

Chapter 7: Why Richard Dawkins Should Believe in Jesus Christ

Phillip Brown

The most popular book written by the New Atheists is Richard Dawkins' *The God Delusion.*[1] I remember distinctly thinking when I saw the bold book cover: Am I deluded? I had better check this out. So I bought the book and looked quickly at the contents to see which chapters would be most important to read first; I did not have the initial patience to wade through the 400 pages to see if I was delusional. I saw in the Contents page, Chapter 3, 'Arguments for God's Existence'. This was the chapter I wanted to begin with. You see, I am personally convinced that God is real. So convinced, in fact, that I have based my entire life solely on that belief. I quickly scanned down the sub-headings in the chapter and turned to page 92, 'Arguments From Scripture'. I did this because I believed that it was fundamentally clear that Jesus Christ was a real historical person. Furthermore, the accounts about Jesus presented within the Bible could be trusted and relied on as accurate historical accounts. But had I missed something? Was I about to be corrected by this brilliant Oxford biologist? Well as it turned out, not even slightly.

Dawkins Thinks Jesus Was Mistaken

Dawkins begins his disregarding of the Bible by stating that *'some people are still persuaded by scriptural evidence to believe in God'.*[2] I am one of these people, and I initially felt intimidated: what was he going to say about me? As it turned out he did not speak about me in so many words, but rather someone else, who like me was persuaded that the Bible was a historical account and could be trusted as evidence that God existed. That person was Clive Staples Lewis, perhaps the most influential Christian in the last 100 years. As Dawkins turned his attention to C S Lewis and his acceptance of scripture as historical, I picked up something quite unsavoury in his writing. Before drawing any conclusions about the Bible and C. S. Lewis' assessment of it, Dawkins ridicules Lewis. He writes, 'a common argument, attributed among others to Lewis (**who should have known better**).[3] Now, being an admirer of C. S. Lewis', it is clear to me why Dawkins is keen to scorn him at the outset. Lewis was an academic, novelist, literary critic, medievalist, essayist, lay theologian and Christian apologist.[4] He was an academic few could match, gaining a triple first from Oxford and publishing books in a wide variety of areas, which have been translated into over thirty languages. How could the God Hypothesis have deluded such a brilliant man? Undoubtedly, Dawkins wants his readers to believe it did and Lewis of all people should not have fallen for such a patent delusion.

What was this mistake that Lewis made about the Bible? Dawkins turns to Lewis' famous argument: if 'Jesus claimed to be the Son of God, he must have been either right or else insane or a liar: 'Mad, Bad or God'. Or, with artless alliteration, 'Lunatic, Liar or Lord'.[5] Dawkins mocks Lewis by attacking the English professor's use of alliteration—clearly he thinks as little of Lewis's language as of his reasoning. Rather than feeling offended by this attack on Lewis' poetic skill, I found myself almost laughing out loud. If you're going to poke fun at bad alliteration, don't use bad alliteration yourself!

Whilst Dawkins' scorn of Lewis backfires he does make a point that needs to be addressed. The point he makes caused me to laugh even harder: Dawkins suggests that Lewis misses a fourth option in his artless alliteration, which is 'that Jesus was honestly mistaken'.[6] Or to put it in Lewis-like alliteration: Lunatic, Liar, Lord or *Lost*. Now let us consider Dawkins' solution to Lewis' puzzle. Dawkins wants his readers to believe that for three adult years of his life, Jesus thought and taught that he was God but he was just simply wrong, and this does not qualify him as a mentally ill, just mildly mistaken. Is Dawkins actually being serious? A man thinks he is God for three years of his adult life and Dawkins wants us to conclude, well he just got it wrong?[7]

Let's consider this proposition in present-day situation. Just imagine you asked your good friend to come over for coffee and a good chat. When you served her coffee, however, she refused to believe that it was coffee but kept saying it was tea. Now on a first visit this would be awkward in and of itself, but if this same event happened over and over for three consecutive years, how could you view your friend as anything other than crazy? Would any reasonable person think that his friend did not have a serious disorder that rendered her incapable or judging reality (if only of coffee and tea) correctly? This is exactly what Dawkins wants you to deduce when assessing the claims of Jesus Christ within scripture. Dawkins wants us to diagnose somebody who routinely makes a mistake about his identity as God for three consecutive years, as just wrong, not crazy. Is that really it? Is that the basis of C. S. Lewis' delusion? Surely not. There must be more.

Sadly there is not, and Dawkins' argument is severely lacking. 'Honestly mistaken' is just not something any honest person can apply to Jesus Christ. Perhaps the weakness of Dawkins argument is the reason why he aggressively discredits the Gospels, and famous people who find them convincing. Dawkins goes on to reinforce this point with another example.

Following on in Chapter 3, 'Arguments for God's Existence' Dawkins states that professor G. A. Wells of the University of London mounts a serious claim that the historical Jesus did in fact not exist.

Dawkins fails to mention that Professor Wells is *not* a professor of history, religion, theology, philosophy, literature, or even anthropology-- all subjects that we would be expect him to be an expert in. Rather, Professor Wells is the Emeritus Professor of German at Birkbeck, University of London. While Wells does hold a degree in Philosophy, his primary field is Language. Why does Dawkins mention Wells' professorship but fail to mention that his field doesn't fit him for assessing the legitimacy of historical figures? The answer seems to be that Dawkins again wants very much to find a professor who asserts that Jesus never existed. Interestingly, in the next paragraph Dawkins does claim that Jesus probably existed,[8] in effect showing that he finds Prof Wells' arguments unconvincing. Dawkins wants to discredit Jesus Christ's existence and the scriptures, but offers little in the way of evidence.

To Dawkins' credit he does make a more serious and robust claim that the accounts of Jesus cannot be entirely historical. This claim concerns the census order by governor Quirinius at the time of Jesus' birth, referred to in the 'Gospel according to Luke'.

Are the Gospels History? - The Census of Quirinius in Luke

Dawkins looks at the alleged problem of the reality of the census depicted in the beginning of Luke's gospel by stating that Luke *'screws up his dating by tactlessly mentioning events that historians are capable of independently checking'.*[9] Below is the passage Dawkins refers to (which he fails to include) in full from the Bible (English Standard Version).

> In those days a decree went out from Caesar Augustus that all the world should be registered. This was the first registration when Quirinius was governor of Syria. And all went to be registered, each to his own town. And Joseph also went up from Galilee, from the town of Nazareth, to Judea, to the city of David, which is called Bethlehem, because he was of the house and lineage of David, to be registered with Mary, his betrothed, who was with child. And while they were there, the time came for her to give birth. And she gave birth to her firstborn son and wrapped him in swaddling cloths and laid him in a manger, because there was no place for them in the inn.[10]

Now there are many Christians who do not have a problem with the little phrase *'first registration when Quirinius was governor of Syria'* in the Gospel of Luke, and most pew-sitters gloss over this detail, not realising that there might be a problem at all. While Dawkins says that Luke 'screws up' the history, he does not deal fully with the issue of the census either. Moreover, Dawkins does not even attempt to engage with modern biblical scholarship on this issue to see what they might have to say about it. Remarkably, Darrell L. Bock's commentary on Luke devotes an entire chapter to this very problem.[11] Why has this famed scientist not looked at all the evidence available to him?

Bock presents the problem of the Quirinius like this:

1. Nothing (outside of the Bible) is known about a general wide census at the time of Augustus.
2. A Roman census would not require people to go to their place of birth.
3. Josephus [The Jewish historian] records no census before the Quirinian census in AD 6. Moreover this census was described in his account as an innovation (suggesting there's no precedent).
4. There would be no census in Palestine in the time of Herod 'The Great'.
5. At the time of the Gospel of Luke's subject, Quirinus could not have been the governor, since the governors' records of that time are well known, and he is not one of them.[12]

Like Dawkins, many atheists (and agnostics) see this apparent historical flaw as a clear example of a historical error in the Gospel of Luke, and sufficient grounds to reject the gospel, and the Bible as a whole, as historically accurate. Dawkins even declared: '*Sophisticated Christians do not need George Gershwin to convince them that 'The things that you're li'ble /To read in the Bible /It ain't necessarily so'*'. However, it seems that Dawkins' failure to consult sophisticated Christians on this very subject makes him liable to dismiss any intelligent answer to this apparent census problem. Let us look at what Bock has to say on the problem.

Objection 1. Nothing is known about a general wide census at the time of Augustus.

Answer 1. [There is historical evidence] that Augustus actually instituted three censuses in this period (See Corbishley 1936 for more).[13] Furthermore, other census cycles existed in Spain and Syria at the same time. Therefore it is not unlikely that Augustus could have issued this decree. The lack of evidence apart from the Bible to corroborate this does not mean the census was a fake.

Objection 2. A Roman census would not require people to go to their place of birth.

Answer 2. It is widely known that Roman law oftentimes permitted local Jewish customs to remain in conjunction with their own laws. Pliny The Younger makes this clear in his letters.[14] Therefore a Jewish desire to be registered in their family's place of origin might plausibly have been added to the Roman imposition of the census.

Objection 3. Josephus [The Jewish historian] records no census before the Quirinian census in AD 6. Moreover, this census was described in this account as an innovation, suggesting there's no precedent.

Answer 3. Even though Josephus is known not to have included this census in his historical analysis, there is strong evidence that imperial representatives could register the emperor's citizens. One example is when taxes in Samaria were reduced by one-quarter at the beginning of Archelaus's rule, a concession that suggests Roman tax roles existed before Samaria became part of a Roman province in an area that had been under the rule of Herod. Therefore it is very possible that Josephus was not privy to the imperial representatives' decision to hold a census.

The problem with the census being an innovation appears to be significant. However, there are some underlying assumptions that are not clear. (If this was the first census) the revolt mentioned by Josephus may have arisen as a response to it. This is not established, however. Hoehner suggests that a census based on Jewish customs would not elicit any reaction from the Jews, although a Roman census based on Roman customs would. Clearly the census in AD 6 had a strong Roman flavour to it, with the unpopular Archelaus at the helm. A Roman census would anger people opposed to Rome. So while it may be that this was the first census, to link a revolt to it on the grounds of novelty seems very unlikely. A more likely conjecture is that the census was an innovation by Roman standards, thus leaving much room for a Jewish-custom based census previously. It should be noted at this point that Luke is trustworthy on matters that we can check.

Objection 4. There would be no census in Palestine in the time of Herod 'The Great'.

Answer 4. See Answer 2.

Objection 5. Quirinius could not have been the governor at that time since the governors' records of that time are well known and he is not one of them.

Answer 5. This is perhaps the hardest of all the objections to answer as there are varied perspectives on it. To me the most plausible is that Quirinius was a legate between Varus and Gaius Caesar in BC 4 – BC 1. Sherwin-White makes this argument based on the governorship gap present in the historical data.[15] The problem here is that it makes the governorship too late for Luke's account. It would be possible if Varus began a census and it was finished under Quirinius, however. This construction would bring the data together. Clearly it is possible because such a census would take a great deal of time to organise. This is a possibility, and the dates do align completely.

Consequently, the only problem with Luke's account of the Quirinius census is that we cannot accurately connect the internal data with the external. But as all history students know, silence on a subject does not necessarily equate to historical fraud. This is perhaps the strongest of Dawkins' arguments against the historical reliability of Jesus Christ, yet it rests on an assumed argument of silence. This is far too weak to make the claim that Luke's gospel cannot be trusted.

Dawkins completes his examination of the arguments from scripture by raising three more objections about the reliability of the texts themselves. He quotes Tom Flynn on the contradictions presented within the Christmas stories in the Gospels of Matthew and Luke. As another chapter will deal with this specific issue, I will not address it here.

Dawkins then introduces the name of Bart Ehrman and his work *Misquoting Jesus*,[16] which argues that the original accounts written in Greek are not what we read in our English translations of the Bible.

Dawkins simply states that these arguments exist, and does not even cite them, and since he does not deal with them we shall not either.

Lastly, Dawkins cites the canonicity of the scriptures—that is, the way in which the Gospels were compiled together—as a problem for reliability. He does this by explaining that there are other Gospels that are not included in our modern Bibles. The Gospel of Thomas is but one example. Dawkins argues that

> The gospels that didn't make it were omitted by those ecclesiastics perhaps because they included stories that were even more embarrassingly implausible than those in the four canonical ones. The Gospel of Thomas, for example, has numerous anecdotes about the child Jesus abusing his magical powers in the manner of a mischievous fairy, impishly transforming his playmates into goats, or turning mud into sparrows.[17]

Again this is just an amateurish understanding of the Gospel of Thomas, and the reasons it does not have a permanent home in our English translations of the scriptures. For one thing, there are two gospels attributed to Thomas, one known as the Coptic Gospel of Thomas and the other known as the Infancy Gospel of Thomas. Clearly Dawkins is referring to the latter, though he does not specify.

As to why the Infancy gospel of thomas is not included in our current Bible, the criteria are far more sophisticated than Dawkins gives credit for. There are many reasons why this Gospel is rejected as an accurate record of Jesus' life. One is that the lack of familiarity with Jewish life and customs suggests very strongly that the apostle did not write this account. Furthermore, the account strongly contradicts that of Luke describing the reaction of the Nazarenes towards Jesus when he performed miracles in close proximity to them. Likewise the ancient church fathers Irenaeus, Origen and Hippolytus include the work in their lists of books they consider heretical. These reasons have nothing to do with Dawkins' argument about its exclusion, nor does he deal with these well-known facts.

Perhaps his most amazing claim, however, is that within the Infancy Gospel of Thomas we have a picture of Jesus that is at odds with the other four Gospels. The Thomas account gives us a picture of a spiteful Jesus, extremely quick tempered, something the other four Gospels just do not allow. This alone should be strong evidence that this is a piece of ancient literature and Christian missionary propaganda, but not an eyewitness account.

And that was it! Dawkins is finished with his analysis of scripture as proof that there is not a God. Dawkins has not done a thorough enough job, either to try and persuade any serious person of the falsity of Jesus, or to actually deal with the historical questions he is trying to address. I can only conclude that it is Dawkins who is trying to delude here, and that he himself is not free from delusion.

---

[1] Richard Dawkins, *The God Delusion*, (London: Bantam Press, 2006).

[2] Ibid., p.92.

[3] Ibid., p.92. My emphasis added.

[4] Douglas Gresham, *Jack's Life: The Life Story Of C.S. Lewis.* (Nashville: Broadman and Holman, 2005).

[5] Dawkins, *The God Delusion* 92.

[6] Ibid.

[7] Mt 4:3, 8:29, 14:33, 16:16, 26:63, 27:4; Mk 1:1, 3:11, 5:7, 15:39, Lk 1:32, 4:3, 4:41, 8:28, 22:70; Jn 1:34, 1:49, 3:18, 10:36, 11:4, 20:31.

[8] Dawkins, *The God Delusion*, 97.

[9] Ibid., 94.

[10] The English Standard Version. Harper Collins. 2002, 1032.

[11] Darrell L. Bock, *Luke 1:1-9:50*, Baker exegetical Commentary on the New Testament (Grand Rapids: Baker Academic, 1994).

[12] Ibid., 903-909.

[13] T. Corbishley, *Quirinius and the Census: A Re-study of the Evidence*, Kilo, 1936.

[14] Letters of Pliny. Author: Pliny Translated by William Melmoth [revised by F. C. T. Bosanquet] see, http://promo.net/pg.

[15] Cited in Bock, *Luke 1:1-9:50*, 903-909.
[16] Dawkins, *The God Delusion*, 95.
[17] Ibid., 96.

Chapter 8: The New Atheists and Philosophical Proof

Phillip Brown

The New Atheists and the Philosophy of Thomas Aquinas

In a previous chapter I explored Richard Dawkins' rather sloppy attempt to persuade people that the Bible cannot be used as evidence that Jesus Christ was God. We may forgive him for this, considering that he is not trained in the field. But what about other academic disciplines that have been co-opted as evidence for God's existence? What about the philosophical arguments from ages past that now-deceased famous men have given for belief in the divine?[1]

Dawkins opens Chapter 3 of *The God Delusion* with an analysis of philosophical and historical arguments for the existence of God. He begins his exploration with Thomas Aquinas' five ways [proofs] of God's existence, presented in his *Summa Theologica*. Aquinas was an Italian Catholic theologian, and has influenced much of Western thought on the matter. Aquinas was a confident believer in the God of the Bible, and wrote much on that belief. His five proofs are a philosophical defence of why we must believe in God, and why it is simply rationally unsound not to do so.

However, as with the arguments from scripture, Dawkins approaches the philosophical arguments misunderstanding what Thomas Aquinas actually wrote. Here is how Dawkins sums up Aquinas' first proof of God:

> The first three are just different ways of saying the same thing, they can be considered together. All involve infinite regress ... and so *ad infinitum*.

The Unmoved Mover. Nothing is caused by itself. Every effect has a prior cause, and again we are pushed back into regress. Something has to make the first move, and that something we call God.[2]

Now, it is not uncommon to condense arguments, particularly philosophical ones, for the purposes of discussion; but if you do it is imperative that you first understand the argument correctly. As will become clear, Dawkins has misunderstood Aquinas, and as a result his summary of his proofs is mistaken. Consequently his pre-emptive answer is also incorrect.

Here is what Thomas Aquinas actually wrote.

The first and more manifest way is the argument from motion. It is certain, and evident to our senses, that in the world some things are in motion. Now whatever is in motion is put in motion by another, for nothing can be in motion except if it is in potentiality to that towards which it is in motion; whereas a thing moves inasmuch as it is in act. For motion is nothing else than the reduction of something from potentiality to actuality. But nothing can be reduced from potentiality to actuality, except by something in a state of actuality. Thus that which is actually hot, as fire, makes wood, which is potentially hot, to be actually hot, and thereby moves and changes it. Now it is not possible that the same thing should be at once in actuality and potentiality in the same respect, but only in different respects. For what is actually hot cannot simultaneously be potentially hot; but it is simultaneously potentially cold. It is therefore impossible that in the same respect and in the same way a thing should be both mover and moved, i.e. that it should move itself. Therefore, whatever is in motion must be put in motion by another. If that by which it is put in motion be itself put in motion, then this also must needs be put in motion by another, and that by another again. But this cannot go on to infinity, because then there would be no first mover, and, consequently, no other mover; seeing that subsequent movers move only inasmuch as they are put in motion by the first mover; as the staff moves only because it is put in motion by the hand. Therefore it is necessary to arrive at a first mover, put in motion by no other; and this everyone understands to be God.[3]

The first thing to notice is that while Aquinas uses the word 'motion', he defines this word to be more closely related to change. The significance is in the description of potentiality and actuality. Changing from cold to hot with burning wood makes this plain. This is not just simple causation or the prime mover, as Dawkins tries to formulate it. Rather it is a sophisticated argument, that if something is going to change from potential to actual then there must have been something in the past that was never potential but eternally actual. The second thing to notice is that Aquinas thinks that infinite regress is impossible at the outset. Aquinas does not position God as a terminator of infinite regress in his first proof, but rather suggests that a first cause is the cause of everything else that we can see. If we do not have a first cause, or an eternal actual being, then what is to stop infinite regress?

Since Aquinas thinks infinite regress is impossible he suggests that there should be a first changer that is itself unchangeable. Aquinas argues rather clearly that for anything to effect 'change' on something else it must have that initial property, *from potentiality to actuality only by something else which is already actualised.*

Here Aquinas is making what we now call the Kalam Cosmological argument. The argument runs like this: Everything that has a beginning must have a cause. Since the general consensus among cosmologists at present is that the universe had a beginning, then there must have been a cause for that beginning. That cause had to have been God.

Recently, one of the smartest people on our planet and the most famous scientist, Stephen Hawking (also an atheist), co-authored a book about what caused the beginning of the universe. *The Grand Design* is an attempt to show that Aquinas' philosophical argument is wrong, and that science clearly holds the answer to how the universe began.[4] Again, however, Hawking makes errors on the same scale as Dawkins in trying to show how this is so. For example, Hawking claims that, 'Because of the Law of Gravity the Universe can and will create itself out of nothing', in opposition to Aquinas.[5] But notice the philosophical problem with this sentence: How can the universe come from nothing and the Law of

Gravity at the same time? Surely the law of gravity is something? What does Hawking mean by 'nothing' when a law of gravity fits into that definition? As you can see even the most eminent scientist cannot throw Aquinas' proof out the window easily, if at all.

But if we go back to Dawkins for the present, we see that not only does he fail to answer Aquinas' first proof, it is obvious that he himself either does not comprehend what Aquinas is arguing, or he has committed intellectual fraud by deliberately misrepresenting what Aquinas wrote. Either explanation raises the question of how Dawkins can be trusted with anything in *The God Delusion*.

In a similar vein Michael Shermer, who is loosely allied with the New Atheists, and author of *How We Believe, Science, Skepticism, and the Search For God* offers some counter-arguments to the existence of God, and attacks Aquinas in the same fashion.[6] His first counter-argument seems weak. Here is Shermer summing up Aquinas:

> Premise 1: The universe moves.
> Premise 2: Everything that moves needs a mover.
> Conclusion: God moves the universe.

Now, as you can see Shermer has made the same mistake as did Dawkins when he condensed Aquinas' argument. Even worse is Shermer's answer to Aquinas. He writes:

> Premise 1: The universe is everything that is, was and shall be.
> Premise 2: God must be in the universe.
> Conclusion: God cannot move the universe because He [God] must need someone to move Him as He is the universe.

It would appear that Shermer's answer *to* Aquinas is sillier and more full of assumptions than his original wrong assertion. As I have shown, Aquinas laboured to describe how we need something fully self-actualised to start the universe. Here Shermer simply ignores Aquinas' argument and puts God back into the universe. And so with a word play he appears to defeat Aquinas. That is, unless you take the time to read Aquinas and understand his initial argument.

Daniel Dennett is no better when looking at Aquinas' argument, re-packaged as the Cosmological Argument. He writes: 'The Cosmological Argument, which in its simplest form states that since everything must have a cause the universe must have a cause—namely God—doesn't stay simple for long.'[7] Dennett, as a trained philosopher, makes the same mistake as Dawkins and Shermer. Both Aquinas and the new Kalam Cosmological Argument make the distinction that it is not a simpler form to say that everything must have a cause. Rather, it is an entirely different argument. The Cosmological Argument is better defined as an argument type looking at facts about the world (*cosmos*) and inferring a logical (*logos*) basis from them.

Dennett wants his readers to think the cosmological argument is a simple one, but it isn't. The argument cannot be reduced to 'everything must have a cause'. Rather, only what we see in the universe (cosmos) needs a cause. Consequently what we see in the universe—the fact that it's expanding and speeding up—implies that we need a cause for it. Or, as Aquinas eloquently puts it, something that is actualised already.

The New Atheists and the historical philosophy of Jesus Christ

While I think Aquinas' proof has many merits, it is not itself as profoundly convincing to me as the resurrection of Jesus Christ. Personally, the truth of Christianity rests alone on the shoulders of Jesus Christ, his historical reality and his claims that he will die and rise again from the dead, thus proving he was and is God. If any of these claims were proven to be false, then I would walk away from Christianity and the ministry I am committed to.

Whilst this fact may not convince other people, especially atheists, there is a strange relationship between their rejection of Jesus' divinity, and the reasons they give for that rock-solid conclusion. The New Atheists in fact do not, and it appears cannot, agree about the historicity of Jesus Christ.

In fact they seem to offer more widely ranging suggestions for his historicity and divinity than any religious person I have ever encountered or read. According to our dictionaries, atheism is a belief or theory that there is no God, but regarding the New Atheists, there is massive discrepancy as to why they believe that Jesus is not God.

Here is but a short list of the New Atheists and the wide-ranging conclusions that they draw regarding Jesus Christ: David Mills thinks '*Jesus probably did not exist*'.[8] Richard Dawkins thinks he probably did exist but was wrong [crazy].[9] Dan Barker thinks Jesus is a '*legend*'.[10] Michel Onfray thinks Jesus is a '*construction*'.[11] Victor Stenger decides Jesus is '*myth*' though it may be based on a real person.[12] John Loftus thinks Jesus was a real man, just not God.[13] Daniel Dennett implies that Jesus is just a meme theory.[14] Michael Martin bases his assessment on G. A. Wells and concludes that Jesus was not a historical person.[15] The late Christopher Hitchens thought that Jesus was just biblical fiction.[16]

Now this should make anyone suspicious of the New Atheists, because they draw one certain conclusion about Jesus Christ (he was not God if he was a real person) based on a wide variety of reasons. Only one of the reasons given by the New Atheists can be correct concerning who or what Jesus Christ was, which means most of them are wrong as to why Jesus should be dismissed as God.

Most, if not all, of the New Atheists are wrong in their reasoning as to why Jesus Christ is not God, then their conclusions as to Jesus Christ should be regarded as highly doubtful. If this were a scientific experiment, would a group of scientists all side with the same conclusion, when varying methods at reaching that conclusion were in direct conflict with each other? The answer is no, they would try and come to a consensus about which methodology is most valid for that conclusion, or they would abandon the conclusion! As a group, then, the New Atheists present to the world evidence that their disbelief in God (specifically the Christian God revealed through the life and ministry of Jesus Christ) is not based on rationality or empirical evidence, but rather gut assumptions. It would be more accurate for them to label themselves the New Agnostics, as this is what they show themselves to be.

The Dubious History of Richard Carrier Concerning Christianity

So, if the resurrection of Jesus is so important, what are the New Atheists saying about it? To consider this, we need to turn to Richard Carrier's *Not the Impossible Faith* and take an in-depth look at *his* argument.[17] Carrier is an historian and an avid atheist in the manner of the New Atheists. He writes in response to a work by J. P. Holding, *The Impossible Faith*. Holding claims that belief in Jesus Christ is only possible if it is true (something I also adhere to). Carrier writes to counter Holding's argument that no-one would believe in a resurrected God unless it had actually happened. In his first paragraph, Carrier suggests that Holding's question *'Who on earth would believe a religion centered on a crucified man?'*[18] can be answered simply by looking and the so-called Babylonian Queen God, Inanna, who according to Carrier was stripped naked and crucified, yet rose again and, triumphant, condemned to Hell her lover.[19]

Whilst this sounds plausible a quick check of Carrier's sources shows they're secondary and far from solid—something any historian should regard with suspicion. What's more when I looked at the The Sumerian text *Inanna's Descent to the Netherworld* or the Akkadian parallel *Ishtar's Descent*. I found Carrier's summary to be completely off-base. Here is a summary of the *Descent of Inanna* myth from the *Encyclopedia of Religion* (edited by Mircea Eliade: cited by Phil Vaz).

> Inanna, the queen of heaven, sought to extend her power over the underworld, ruled by her sister, Ereshkigal. As in the Akkadian text, Inanna descends through seven gates, at **each removing an article of clothing or royal regalia until, after passing through the seventh gate, she is naked and powerless.** She is killed and her corpse hung on a hook. Through a stratagem planned before her descent, she is revived, but she may not return above unless she can find a substitute to take her place. She re-ascends, accompanied by a force of demons who will return her to the land of the dead if she fails. After allowing two possible candidates to escape, she comes to Erech, where Dumuzi, the shepherd

king who is her consort, appears to be rejoicing over her fate. She sets the demons on him, and after he escapes several times, he is captured, killed, and carried off to the underworld to replace Inanna. ("Dying and Rising Gods", volume 4, page 525-6, emphasis mine).[20]

As Phil Vaz points out, Carrier's emphasis (in bold) has misrepresented the story. Inanna is not stripped naked and crucified; rather she descended to the underworld slowly removing her clothing piece by piece and at which point she was killed! Carrier even acknowledges that Holding knows that Inanna was not crucified, and simply restates his point: 'Holding has tried to protest that Inanna wasn't really crucified. But being stripped naked, killed, and nailed up in shame amounts to the same thing to any reasonable observer'.[21]

What should be made of Carrier's first rebuttal against Holding? Was he aware of his sources, but chose to ignore them, or was he unaware and chose not to follow through on Holding's original protest? Either way it leaves Carriers point running afoul of significance.

Carrier then moves on to a direct discussion the cult of Attis (in support of people following a disgraced king—a eunuch in this case, the castrated Attis) but we can leave this aside, knowing that Carrier has not refuted Holding.[22]

Carrier marks a continuation of the disgraced king worship, in which he argues that 'the early Christians appear to have come from disgruntled poor or middle class, who had grown disgusted with the fundamental injustices in their society and government'. (Carrier Page 24) Carrier cites the desire of the Apostle Paul—in the Book of Acts—to support this point. Interestingly enough however, Paul himself did not fit this mould, being an upper class Jew, with impeccable credentials, at the forefront of justice to his people (Christians). Furthermore Luke, the physician, therefore not poor but upper middle class, does not fit this model either. How can Carrier argue that possible desires trump actual accounts? Again, what are we to make of Carrier's point here? It's as if some major details escape his methodology.

Whilst Carrier does make some sound observations—that Christianity did find strength in the poor and oppressed—and Holding does have some oversimplifications to address, clearly it cannot be as Carrier attempts to suggest. To illustrate this point completely (on page 34) Carrier argues that many people expected a humiliated savior.[23] Carrier feels confident to make this point because the scripture, the Old Testament, says that plainly. This point Carrier thinks is a reasonable claim to assume that at best a large number of people had been prepared by Jewish scriptures to expect that someone would suffer a most humiliation execution at the hands of the wicked elite, despite his complete innocence and that this person would be the Chosen One of God, a Son of God.[24]

Not only is this the only piece of evidence that Carrier gives to support his argument, but he fails to consider a whole range of evidence against this possibility. First, for Carrier's point to hold water, he must show that these texts he refers to are in line with what was actually taught in the first century Jewish synagogue, something a trained historian should be able to accomplish. Second, if Carrier cannot present data to confirm this, he must show teaching in line with that text (as presenting texts as evidence does nothing to show authority or adherence for an illiterate culture). Third, Carrier must give evidence as to why Alfred Edersheim, in *The Life and Times of Jesus the Messiah* is wrong to argue:

> It were an extremely narrow, and, indeed, false view, to regard the difference between Judaism and Christianity as confined to the question of the fulfillment of certain prophecies in Jesus of Nazareth. These predictions could only outline individual features in the Person and history of the Messiah. It is not thus that a likeness is recognised, but rather by the combination of the various features into a unity, and by the expression which gives it meaning. So far as we can gather from the Gospel narratives, no objection was ever taken to the fulfillment of individual prophecies in Jesus. But the general conception which the Rabbis had formed of the Messiah, differed totally from what was presented by the Prophet of Nazareth. Thus, what is the fundamental divergence between the two may be said to have existed long before the

events which finally divided them. It is the combination of letters which constitute words, and the same letters may be combined into different words. Similarly, both Rabbinism and—what, by anticipation, we designate—Christianity might regard the same predictions as Messianic, and look for their fulfillment; while at the same time the Messianic ideal of the Synagogue might be quite other than that, to which the faith and hope of the Church have clung.[25]

Carrier continually points to faults in Holding's research, but does no better, in my opinion. This chapter is not a careful rebuttal of Holding; it is a one-sided, ill-considered rhetorical snap at Holding, and casts long shadows over the rest of this work and the money paid to produce it. It becomes increasingly clear then, when we look closely at the philosophical and historical rigor of the New Atheists, that they actually make disbelief impossible to believe.

---

[1] We can think of philosophy as the study on the nature of reality and knowledge.

[2] Richard Dawkins, *The God Delusion*. (London: Bantam Press, 2006), 77.

[3] Thomas Aquinas, *Summa Theologica*, (Christian Classics, 1981).

[4] Stephen Hawking and Leonard Mlodinow, *The Grand Design*. (London: Bantam Press, 2010).

[5] Ibid., 180.

[6] Michael Shermer, *How We Believe: Science, Skepticism, and the Search for God*. 2nd ed., (New York: Holt Paperbacks, 2003).

[7] Daniel C. Dennett, *Breaking the Spell: Religion as Natural Phenomenon* (London: Penguin Books, 2006), 242.

[8] David Mills, *Atheist Universe: The Thinking Person's Answer to Christian Fundamentalism*, (Berkeley: Ulysses Press, 2006), 45.

[9] Dawkins., 97.

[10] Dan Barker, *Godless: How an Evangelical Preacher Became One of America's Leading Atheists*, (Berkeley: Ulysses Press, 2008), 251.

[11] Michel Onfray, *The Atheist Manifesto: The Case Against Christianity, Judaism and Islam*, (Melbourne: Melbourne University Press, 2007), 115.

[12] Victor J. Stenger, *God: the Failed Hypothesis: How Science Shows That God Does Not Exist*, (New York: Prometheus Books, 2007), 181.

[13] John W. Loftus, *Why I Became an Atheist: A Former Preacher Rejects Christianity*, (New York: Prometheus Books, 2008), 317.

[14] Dennett, *Breaking the Spell: Religion as Natural Phenomenon*, (London: Penguin Books, 2006), 141-147.

[15] Michael Martin, *The Case Against Christianity* (Philadelphia: Temple University Press, 1993), 67.

[16] Christopher Hitchens, *God Is Not Great*, (New York: Twelve, 2007), 111-112.

[17] Richard Carrier, *Not the Impossible Faith* (Raleigh: Lulu.com, 2009).

[18] Ibid., 17.

[19] Ibid.

[20] Phil Vaz, 'The Evidence for Jesus: on Inanna (Ishtar) "Crucifixion" and Zalmoxis "Resurrection," http://www.philvaz.com/apologetics/JesusEvidenceCarrier.htm Accessed May 27, 2011.

[21] Carrier, *Not the Impossible Faith*, p.19.

[22] Ibid., 20.

[23] The title of the last section in chapter 1. Ibid., 34.

[24] Ibid., p.43.

[25] Alfred Edersheim, *The Life and Times of Jesus the Messiah.* (Peabody: Hendrickson, 1988).

Chapter 9: Six Days?

Tim Patrick

The Unbridgeable (?) Gulf

One of the issues that has long fueled the 'science vs faith' debates is around the age of the earth. At the popular level, two camps are pretty clearly marked out. There are the serious Christians who believe that the Bible, specifically its opening chapter, Genesis 1, teaches that the world was made over six consecutive twenty-four hour days.[1] Then, there are those unbelievers who place more trust in the 'rational scientific world-view' and therefore accept the weight of the physical, geological and biological data that point us towards an age for the earth of the order of 5 billion years, with the universe being around 15 billion years old. To continue the no-too-fanciful characterisation, the Christian camp then believes that to reject the plain teaching of the Bible is tantamount to rejecting God himself. And because of this, some of them have taken belief in six-day creation as a simple litmus test for the state of a person's faith. Disbelieve it and you're closed to God. On the other hand, the rationalistic atheists think that to ignore the plain evidence of the natural sciences is to dispense with reason and even commonsense. Therefore, Christians who hold to a six-day creation are brainless loons who take ancient fairy tales far too seriously—sometimes dangerously far.

And so the battle lines are drawn.

Sometimes (often quite embarrassingly in my view) Christians try to prove their six-day time frame scientifically by showing how those working in the mainstream sciences have failed to interpret the natural data correctly. They look at things like strange fossils and deep-space background radiation and then present explanations of how these phenomena came to be within a six-day creation and a six-thousand-year-old earth. But few who have formal training in the natural sciences find any of this particularly convincing. In fact, these attempts at demonstrating the reasonableness of young-earth-creation often only serve to confirm the view that Bible-believing Christians are miles out of touch with reality.

Another sad thing that often happens is that the debate is held at a very poor standard. There regularly isn't proper engagement between equally learned opponents, but instead lots of cheap shots and second-hand arguments are thrown about with advocates of both positions preaching to the converted (or unconverted as the case may be) about the obvious soundness of their own position and the obvious stupidity of the alternative. And so the caricatures continue to be reinforced and the issue continues to grow its own vibrant life that's one or more steps removed from the real questions. When I have the opportunity to speak on this subject, I sometimes ask the audience whether they have actually read through even the popular primary texts like Darwin's *Origin of Species* or Hawking's *A Brief History of Time* or if they've ever engaged in any meaningful study of the opening chapters of Genesis. Usually, few have.

What I want to do in this essay is to turn back to the question as someone who is both a Christian committed to the authority of scripture and a geologist with confidence in the reliability of the scientific method. In doing so, I also want to reject the usual shape of the popular debate. I don't believe it's possible for truth in one sphere to jar with truth in another. If both the Bible and the natural sciences deliver truth, then where there appears to be a clash, it must only be apparent. Furthermore, I suspect it is often not inadequate data that limits our understanding, but rather our failure to think in right categories.

For me, the question rests on a good reading of Genesis 1. I know that as soon as some people read that, they will immediately conclude that I'm a soft or compromised Christian who isn't really serious about the scriptures. However, even in this short chapter, I hope to be able to demonstrate the opposite—that it is my desire to read the text of Genesis 1 seriously, carefully and theologically contextualised in the rest of scripture that leads me to my position. So I don't take Genesis 1 as a literal chronology because *I don't think it was ever intended to be one.* I would even go further and say that I believe there's a real risk of distorting what that text was primarily written to communicate if its six-day structure is taken as being its substance. It would be a bit like receiving an attractively wrapped package at Christmastime and then assuming that the present was the shiny wrapping paper and not what was inside.

For anyone uncomfortable with what I've said so far, I just ask for charity. That is, I'd like to ask you to read through the chapter with an open mind before rejecting it outright. And if you decide that it really doesn't hold water, please be assured that I too want to hold my view humbly enough to welcome correction where I'm demonstrably wrong.

Desires Beyond Knowledge

Before I move to the text of Genesis 1 itself, I want to present a paradigm, that of the *interface*. It will take a few steps to build it up, but think it's a useful starting point.

The very first step is for us all to make an admission. The thing to admit is that when it comes to the very early history of the universe—and especially its pre-history—we're all just guessing. Atheistic scientists and six-day creationists alike need to have peace with this because the reality is that even within each camp's own world-view, there are limits to what can be claimed. The theory of the big-bang is now generally accepted in the astrophysical and broader scientific communities and among the non-religious general population. However, there are lots of things around and about the big-bang that no one has any real idea about. For example, why did the big-bang happen instead of not happen? What was the trigger for the big-bang if nothing existed before it? In what place did the singularity from which the big-bang emanated exist? How long had the singularity existed before the big-bang occurred? Where did the infinitely compressed matter in the singularity come from? I am well aware that some of these are improper and circular questions. That is, we cannot think of time, space and matter in the same way when we are thinking of the pre- and early-history of the universe because different physics was at play. And it neither makes sense to ask where something was before the event that created it nor how long something had existed in the pre-history of time. But my point is simply that even when theoretical and high-energy particle physicists ask these questions in better ways, these are exactly the sorts of questions that they still don't have answers for. When it gets down to discussing the origins of the universe at this level, the data is thin and the guesswork is substantial. Even highly gifted leaders in the field like the famous Stephen Hawking openly admit that in their attempts to make of sense of it all, they can just offer 'proposal[s]' that 'cannot be deduced from some other principle' but which have been 'put forward for aesthetic or metaphysical reasons' and which may be difficult to prove.[2]

Please note that what I'm not trying to do here is prove that the whole scientific case is flimsy. This is not an attempt to discredit good research. The exploration of physical origins is a worthy pursuit and the complex imaginings and theorisings of brilliant minds is the proper business of science which has yielded incredible knowledge that we should be very thankful for. All I want to say is that, at this stage, those brilliant minds are far, far from having all the answers. Again, when it comes to the very early origins of the universe, even the sharpest of us are still guessing.

Of course, Bible-believing Christians are in precisely the same place. When we look at the very first verses of Genesis we could ask all the same sorts of questions. Where was God before he spoke the creation into being? How long had he been there? Where did he come from? How long had the 'waters' of Genesis 1, verse 2 been there? And so on and so on. Again, we simply have no answers. We either descend into *reductio ad absurdum* or else halt the conversation by saying something like, 'God was and he was sovereign and that's sufficient'. There's a level at which I believe that, but there's also a level at which it's just a dodge. In my view, better to start with the humility to admit that there's a lot that we all just don't know and we don't even really have any ideas about how we could know.

In all of this however, it is interesting to note how these questions nag us. The raw fact is that it doesn't really make any practical difference to anyone's life whatsoever if the world was made in six days, six months or six billon years. The elapsed time of creation doesn't have any direct effect on our decision-making, our relationships, our health, our emotions. It's fantastically irrelevant! So why do any of us care at all and why do so many of us care so much?

It is, of course, because of the God question. The real reason that people care about the chronology of creation is not because the time it took matters much to anybody, but because the truth on this question has implications for our beliefs about the existence and nature of God. In addition, I also think that our intrinsic inquisitiveness about the origin of our world and ourselves is something that's inescapably 'human'. Unlike other living things, we understand that where we have come from determines something of who we are and therefore knowing about our past helps us know about ourselves.

So, we find that we are an inquisitive race and we naturally want to learn about our early origins but there is a great deal that lies well beyond our knowing. Both scientists and people of faith (if I can keep making that false distinction for a moment) want to know more than we have ready access to. And that brings us to our next step—and I want to take us there via our computer screens.[3]

The PC Paradigm

One of the great leaps forwards in personal computing was the development of the Graphical User Interface or GUI. Prior to this, people interacted with the data in their computer through lines of text, often coded text. (There are some tech-bods who still compute this way and I always find myself impressed at their ability to decipher the jumbled lines of symbols on their screens.) But since the broad adoption of GUIs, we now interact with our data on a virtual desktop covered in symbolic icons. We have virtual folders, virtual documents, virtual buttons and all the rest. It's so familiar to us that we tend to forget that none of it is real! As we sit in front of our screens, we do things like look into a folder, open one of the documents inside, scroll through the document to a certain point and then go ahead and change the format of the text and so on. It's all very straightforward and intuitive—apart from the fact that we're not really doing what it looks like we're doing at all. Although the folders on my computer look like tiny versions of the folders in my office filing cabinet, there are not really teeny-weeny cardboard folders stored inside my computer. And while the documents on my computer screen look like the printed paper documents in the folders in my filing cabinet, there aren't really any teeny-weeny printed documents hidden inside my computer at all. In my computer, all my data is actually just stored as long chains of 0s and 1s. And, even then, those 0s or 1s are just representations of the ultimate physical reality—vast sequences of microscopic capacitors that have been switched to one of two possible states by small, controlled electrical pulses.[4] My computer screen therefore isn't just a large, rectangular, backlit magnifying glass that allows me to look at and interact with miniaturised folders, documents and photos. It's actually a cleverly designed interface that presents my data and lets me manipulate it in a way that's familiar and makes good sense to me by emulating my real desktop, folders and files. The screen takes what is unknown and unknowable to me and presents it in a form that's plainly meaningful and easily intelligible.

And here's the first key thing about this: *everybody is fully aware of it*. I cannot imagine that the previous paragraph caused anyone who read it to lose their innocence. To tell an adult reader that computer screens are just smart interfaces is not akin to telling a child that there is no Tooth Fairy. The second important thing follows: *no one is angry about this*. That is, no one feels outraged at the computer manufacturers for perpetuating a massive deception on us by hiding the *real* truth about how our data looks and presenting us with just a false representation of it. And of course, the reason we don't, is that the computer makers are doing nothing so sinister. Their goal in giving us GUIs is positive. It's to help us make good and easy use of the data in our computers not to conceal important facts for their own gain. We all know this without needing to think about it and we are thankful for it, not angry at it.

Now we need to bring these pieces together…

An Interface with the Incomprehensible Past

My contention is that Genesis 1 serves not to deceive us inquisitive humans about the real origins of the universe, but to serve as a useful interface for us. It helps us to understand what we really need to understand in order to know who we are in the universe and how we can interact with it in healthy and productive ways. There is plenty of room for the research physicists to keep working out more of the raw, uninterpreted physical history just as there is a need for some people to be able to pull apart a computer and work out what's happening inside. This is all good and necessary for curious creatures who want to keep understanding more of the mechanics. But for most of us (and even for those experts too) the important thing needed for both everyday computer use and for understanding our origins in our universe is a good interface.

In this, I need to be very clear that I am not saying that Genesis 1 is either just a useful legend or a myth. A legend is a story told with the intention that the listeners will receive not just its point but also its details as substantially true, no matter how fantastic they are. On the other hand, a myth is a story generally acknowledged as not being true but shared in order to impart some wisdom, to fill in an unknowable history or just for entertainment. I think Genesis 1 is more like a parable; a story told to communicate a profound idea, but where the setting is understood to be creatively imagined for the purpose.[5] Good examples of parables are George Orwell's *Animal Farm* or many of the well-known stories that Jesus told.

It's worth noting at this point that I also believe the book of Revelation serves much the same function as the last book of the scriptures. Just as limited human beings cannot possibly see into the very early or pre-history of time, neither can we project infinitely into the future. Despite its notoriously complicated imagery, it's widely agreed that Revelation describes the events of the close of time as we know it and the completion of the New Creation.[6] One of the reasons for its dense imagery is that

Revelation draws together many of the images used throughout the entire Bible. (The fact that Revelation is the last book of the Bible gives us the hint that we will understand it best in the context of all that has come before—including the earlier biblical metaphors.) But the other reason is that the things Revelation describes are just beyond the limits of direct human comprehension. So the Bible presents them to us through a vision given to John the Apostle.

Two key points arise out of this observation. The first is that my view of the opening chapter of Genesis gels with a deliberate, overarching shape for the whole Bible metanarrative. That is, it is intended to make sense not just in its own right as we'll explore next, but importantly, it also coheres within the presentation framework of the entire story of the scriptures. The second point— and I cannot emphasise this one enough— is that although I don't believe the very opening and closing chapters of the Bible are intended as literal, chronological histories, I do believe that the vast majority of the Old and New Testament narratives are. I make that determination on both the paradigmatic grounds discussed above and the stylistic grounds discussed below.[7]

Patterns of Order and Perfection in Genesis 1:1-2:3

So far, all that I've presented might seem like a good theory but nothing more. Up to this point I have only been talking *about* Genesis, not actually *reading* any of the text of Genesis itself. This is where we must now turn, focusing on chapter 1 but running through to the end of the section at chapter 2, verse 3.

Obviously, the writer or final redactor of Genesis had no engagement with the world of scientific thought, predating it by some 3,500 years, give or take. Therefore, we can't read what they wrote as any kind of scientific presentation—that would be a terrible anachronism. Rather, it must be read on its own terms.[8]

The first point to make is obvious but important and it is that the chapter does not read like the rest of biblical history or even like a narrative at all.

It's far more poetic. The highly structured passage is so familiar to lots of us that we perhaps forget this. But apart from the important but immeasurable rhythms and mood of the chapter, we can also point to some more concrete stylistic craftsmanship. For starters, there is a recurring pattern within each day -

1. God said, "Let there be ... / Let the ... / Let us make ... "
2. and there was ... / and it was so
3. And God saw that ... was good
4. God called [named] ... (days 1-3 only)
5. And there was evening and there was morning, the ... day.

The pattern is not rigidly tight, but tight enough that the exceptions prove the rule. It captures both the discipline and the freedom of a creative art form.

Beyond this, the six days together fit into a bigger structural pattern.[9]

On the first three days, we see a creation of the different 'spaces' in which things can exist.[10] Then, on the next three days we see each of those spaces in turn being appropriately populated. God names each of the spaces in this chapter but the naming of the animals and birds is delegated to Adam in Genesis 2. We also see the broad growth in complexity of the life forms as we progress forward through the days; from plants to sea creatures to birds to land animals to human beings as the pinnacle of the created order.

Day	Inanimate Creation	Day	Animate Creation
1	Light	4	Sun, moon and stars
2	Sky and sea	5	Aquatic animals and birds
3	Land and vegetation	6	Land animals and people

In addition to the patterning, as we look at the order of events, we also notice things which indicate that we're not reading something meant to be accurate as a scientific piece. One example is that in the Genesis 1 account, light exists before the light sources. I have had someone suggest to me that perhaps this is because in those first days of creation, light didn't originate from the sun or stars as it does today and that there was a switch to that mechanism at some later stage. Apart from the fact that verse 15 of the chapter explicitly says that the sun, moon and stars were made 'to give light upon the earth', in the end such arguments are self-defeating. To posit that originally, light didn't come from the sun is to say that Genesis 1 is not really an account of the creation of the universe we see today. We must be very careful not to push the chapter beyond what it will bear. There is nothing noble in protecting the literal six-day creation thesis *despite what the text itself actually says*. As I said earlier in this chapter, my view is not just that it's possible to read Genesis 1 as non-literal, but that it's actually truer to the text to do so than to force an idea that doesn't really fit the details. The six days is the literary device, not the message.[11]

Of course, none of this should trouble us because there are plenty of other places in the Bible where the creation is spoken of poetically like this without endangering the truth. Psalm 19 comes to mind. Here we read that God made a tent for the sun and that the sun 'rises' and runs across its path like a strong man. We don't read any of this literally because we know exactly what Psalm 19 is talking about and we're not at all worried that this beautiful song of creation is somehow a terrible distortion of the scientific truth.

Returning to the patterns in Genesis 1, another thing that's important to observe is the symbolic use of the number seven. As we think about this, it's first necessary to be clear in what we mean by 'symbolic'. What we certainly don't mean is that seven is used as part of some complicated numerological system (you know, one of the ones where you take your date of birth, multiply it by the street number of your first house, convert it to hexadecimal and divide it by the number of letters in the name of the serving president of the USA...). Nor are we thinking of the 'biblical arithmetic' where people pore over dates in the Bible trying to sum up the exact day when the world started, or when it's going to end. Rather, the symbolic use of a number is just that; taking a number to symbolise an idea. We don't do this a lot in Western societies, although there are a few examples such as 'lucky' 7 or 'unlucky' 13. We know that there's no rational reason to think the number 13 is an omen for bad luck, but it still symbolises that idea for lots of people. Another good example is when we say '110%' as in, 'I support you 110%'. Again, we know that 110% is a nonsense number, but we use it symbolically as an emphatic way of saying 'as much as possible, and then some more too'.

The Israelites who first owned the text of Genesis had other symbolic numbers and seven was one of the most significant. It symbolises divinity—that something is of God. We see this carried right through the Bible to the book of Revelation which is full of sets of seven—seven churches, seven lampstands, seven stars, seven seals, seven trumpets, a seven-headed beast, seven plagues and more too. Probably the best explanation for the beast of Revelation 13 having the number 666 is because he stands as a counterfeit for the true God and, in the same way that six falls short of seven, the beast falls short of the one who is perfect trinity, whose own number would be 777.[12] Also, in Matthew's Gospel, Jesus famously responds to Peter's question as to how many times he needs to forgive another believer who has sinned against him. Jesus says, not just seven times, but seventy times seven. Obviously, the point isn't that a believer is obliged to forgive exactly 490 times, but that they should forgive in a God-like way—repeatedly and completely.

We find the symbolic number seven laced throughout the opening chapter of Genesis. Not only is the passage primarily shaped into seven stanzas around the seven days, but some of its patterns are deliberately culminated at the seventh occurrence. For example, although the creation only actually takes six days, the added day of rest brings the passage up to the perfect number. Similarly, the declaration that creation is 'good' comes six times before the seventh and final declaration that it is 'very good'.[13] We also see a couple of other interesting things when we look at the original Hebrew text from which our English versions are translated.

For example, the two focal words of the passage 'God' and 'Earth' (or 'land', here meaning the 'creation') appear in multiples of seven— thirty-five and twenty-one times respectively. And then, when we come to the seventh and final paragraph, we find that it culminates with three very repetitive consecutive sentences, each centred on the phrase 'the seventh day'.[14]

Conclusion

So for me, the big question that arises from the text of Genesis 1 itself is, did the author write this chapter in this way in order to teach us that God worked on his Creation for six consecutive 24-hour periods or is there something far more significant that he wanted to communicate? Is the real purpose of the passage nothing to do with chronology and everything to do with declaring that the world was purposefully created and created good by the all-powerful and sovereign God of Israel? I think the unambiguous answers from Genesis 1 are yes. And not only are these facts presented in the passage, but the deliberate, careful, artistic crafting of the text also serve to reinforce the explicit points. The creation is divine. It is of God. It carries his stamp all over it. Genesis 1 tells us all this in style as well as content. I deeply value the intention to be faithful to the Bible as the word of God and therefore understand and respect those who want to read Genesis 1 as a straightforward chronology of creation. However, I do feel as though that actually empties the text of some of the force and depth that God gave it.

Having come to this point though, a fair question to ask is, why? If, as I have argued, Genesis 1 is not meant to communicate that God created the world in a literal six-day period, then why did he cause it to be written that way? Why doesn't Genesis 1 say,

> God said, 'Let there be a cosmos', and then, through various processes of physics operating over several billion years, it was so. And God said, 'Let there be an inhabitable planet', and through the action of geological forces operating over millions of years, it was so…

... and so on? Surely this would have been a less confusing way to present the creation story if this is what had actually happened.

I think there are several reasons why Genesis 1 isn't written that way. First of all, few people would understand it. Apart from the well-educated peoples of the past couple of hundred years, most of humanity for most of history wouldn't have been able to make much sense of the concepts of the 'processes of physics' and 'geological forces'. The language chosen for Genesis 1 was the widely-understood creation language of the period when it was written and there would be a whiff of arrogance in us if we were to expect that an ancient book was crafted to best suit our generation's way of understanding things more than those generations before us.[15] If the goal of Genesis 1 is to provide a helpful interface for God's people to make sense of the most important things about their farthest origins, a technical, scientific presentation would overwhelmingly fail to do that.

Following directly on, the second reason is that if Genesis 1 were written that way, it would actually detract from its main points. The focus would shift from the primacy, agency and power of God to the time-periods and natural processes he employed. And repeating what I wrote above, there's nothing at all wrong with universities and laboratories investigating those scientific processes, but that's not where Genesis 1 wants to take our minds. Its goal is not to have us ponder the machinery of creation, but its divinity and the deity of its creator.

Finally, I think a more technical presentation of Genesis would kill the beauty of the passage. I know this is subjective, but that doesn't make it unimportant. Human beings are emotional creatures and it's not just raw facts that resonate within us, but truth presented creatively and beautifully. This might sound like a soft argument, but just consider the size of the music, film and fashion industries for half a moment and it's clear that we are deeply aesthetic creatures.[16] If anybody wants to speak into the human heart, they must use more than sterile data. The so called New Atheists know this only too well even if only subconsciously. Despite their continued appeals to 'reason' and 'rationality', many of their arguments are highly impassioned pieces of rhetoric directed towards their audiences' wills as much as their minds. And many of them are driven to promote atheism because of their underlying emotional concerns as much as any disinterested intellectual convictions.[17] While it is dangerous to not be emotionally self-aware or honest regarding the degree to which our emotions drive our various agendas, being emotional is not at all a bad thing in and of itself—imagine a world full of Mr Spocks! Whole beings are emotional as well as rational. I believe Genesis 1 speaks not just to our minds, but to our whole selves as complex creatures in God's good creation.

My concluding thought on our subject may be surprising although I've already hinted at it. It is that at the end of the day ('end of the day' here meant metaphorically, of course), I'm just not that fussed about it all—to me this is an open-handed issue and I'm comfortable with being proven wrong in my views on it. That is to say, the time-span of Creation is not particularly important to my faith. Or, to put it another way, my faith does not rest on how long I think it took God to create the world. Or another, I don't believe a particular view on the days of Genesis 1 is a central tenet of Christianity. One of my great disappointments is just how much energy this whole 'debate' consumes because it seems to me that it's something of a red herring. The imperative of the Bible is that we come to a view on the identity of Jesus of Nazareth. The primary call of the scriptures is for people made in God's image to follow Jesus as Lord and trust him as saviour, not to believe in a literal six-day creation nor to derive a viable synthesis of Genesis 1 and data generated by the physical sciences. This isn't to say that there aren't important questions to ask about how the world was created or what the author of Genesis 1 intended to communicate, but it does mean that these are not the questions of first importance.

Therefore, while I'm prepared to put some good time and thought into the issues of this essay, I would hope that Christians give a larger proportion of their time to engaging the world around them with the question of Jesus and to showing the love of God through their words and actions. And I would also encourage anyone who isn't a Christian believer to do the same. There's no need to end the conversation around the relationship between science and faith, but it's good to realise that if this is where you stay, you're only ever skirting the fringe of the bigger questions of Christianity and of God. If the world we live in was the work of an all-powerful creator, if he ordered it carefully and gave human beings a special place in it and if it all started out 'very good', then we need to be asking about what happened to it all and how can we, as beings somehow made in the image of the creator, reestablish good, safe, healthy and loving relationships with him. These are the bigger questions and these are the very questions that Jesus came to answer.

Appendix: When does Genesis Change Genre?

As I said in the main body of this essay, while I don't believe that Genesis 1 is intended to be taken as a literal, chronological history of events, I do believe much of the rest of the Bible is. So the question arises, at what point in my paradigm does Genesis shift to that more literal history? Unfortunately, I'm not yet fully resolved on this issue, however, I can point to some important cues in the text of Genesis that I think will help us work towards an answer.

Most serious scholars are agreed that we are certainly in read-it-off-the-page history by the time we reach the Abram narratives starting at Genesis 12. Some would suggest that it's actually at Genesis 12 that the shift occurs. This view might be considered attractive because it quickly deals with many of the texts that are most controversial if treated as histories: Adam, Eve and the Garden of Eden, Noah's Ark and the worldwide flood and the Tower of Babel. However, I'm not sure it can be dealt with so simply. There are real theological problems that arise with this view, not least being what it means if Adam and Eve weren't real people and the Fall wasn't an historical event. There's also the procedural problem of watering down tough texts—if we can allegorise Genesis 1-11, then why not those parts of Exodus that seem historically implausible, or why not the miracles and resurrection of Jesus? But beyond this, even the text itself really doesn't indicate any sort of shift between Genesis 11 and

12. In fact, Abram is first introduced to us in Genesis 11:26 before a genealogy runs us through to the start of Genesis 12. It seems like the author's intention was more that we see direct continuity, not a change of style at this point.

A more fruitful line of investigation might be around the *'elleh toledot* formula. This is a Hebrew phrase meaning 'These are the generations of ...' and it stands as a marker at several points throughout the early chapters of Genesis (2:4, 5:1, 6:9, 10:1, 11:10, 11:27).[18] If the *'elleh toledot* statements stand as headings to the sections that follow them (as I think they must), they serve to divide Genesis 1-11 up into its separate parts. (We must remember that the chapterisation of the Bible is not original and oftentimes obscures the natural divisions of the text.) We might then suggest that the straight historical narrative begins with the first *'elleh toledot* statement at Genesis 2:4, that is, directly after the creation narrative in Genesis 1:1-2:3. This would make the opening chapter of Genesis something akin to a prologue to the narrative of the rest of the book (cf. the prologue in Chapter 1 of John's Gospel which has allusions to Genesis 1). It also makes sense of the fact that we have another account of Creation in Genesis 2, this one being from a more personal perspective like the rest of the *'elleh toledot* sections.

Another possibility is that there is some sort of gear-shift around Genesis 5:1-2. In these verses there is the only variant of the *'elleh toledot* formula (*zeh sefer toledot*: 'This is the book of the generations of ..'.) and a reference back to Genesis 1:27 which is somewhat odd and perhaps signals that chapter 5 is the starting point to a new section of narrative. Certainly, there is a sense of narratival resolution at the end of chapter 4 (even if it is ominous and leaves a situation that will require subsequent attention) and we don't find ourselves struggling for context if we start our reading from chapter 5. In this case, chapters 1-4 might be considered the prologue to the rest of the book.

Again, none of this is definitive, but I hope it might give a few helpful leads for us if we want to take up this question, which arises from our main study.

[1] While this view is not exclusive to Christianity, the present chapter is not aiming to interact with other faiths.

[2] From Stephen Hawking's famous *A Brief History of Time* (London: Transworld Publishers Ltd, 1989), 145. Though positive about the potential of scientific discovery, Hawking's book ends on a very whimsical note. He wonders 'What is it that breathes fire into the equations and makes a universe for them to describe?' and 'Why does the universe go to all the bother of existing?' (page 184). His final paragraph says that if a complete theory–the holy grail of research physics-can ever be worked out, it would merely provide the philosophers, scientists and ordinary people with the starting point for 'the discussion of the question of why it is that we and the universe exist' (page 185). Clearly, he sees that there is a great deal to understand beyond the limits of physics!

[3] I owe this brilliant illustration to Bishop Robert Forsyth.

[4] This is for semiconductor storage. There are other ways we store our data too, such as optically or magnetically.

[5] To complicate things a bit, I think it was God who did the imaging in Genesis 1 because he knew that the six day format would be the most powerful vehicle for the truth he wanted to communicate.

[6] I am of the view that Revelation addresses the entire period between the first and second comings of Jesus.

[7] I offer some thoughts as to when Genesis shifts from non-literal to literal in the appendix.

[8] A more thorough study of Genesis in its own right would need to account for the context in which it was written. However, given that there are many excellent, enlightening studies that discuss the opening chapters of Genesis in the light of its contemporary Ancient Near Eastern creation narratives, I don't want to retread that ground here. Suffice to say that the overlap is considerable and at the very least, these comparisons demonstrate a common thought-world, language and motifs that were used by the writer of Genesis and their contemporaries.

[9] I think this is reasonably well known, but it was first pointed out to me by Tim Hill.

[10] Panning back once more to the overall shape of the Bible, we see complementary and concluding acts of creation in the book of Revelation. We notice that the 'spaces' created in Genesis 1 have constraints. The sun and moon give the light that plants and animals need to see and live, but there is still

darkness too. Similarly, there is land-a refuge from the chaos of the waters-but there are also still seas. But in the New Creation described in Revelation, those limits are removed. There is no more night and no more sun or moon necessary because God and Jesus will be continual sources of light (Rev 21:23-25, 22:5) and the sea will be no more (21:1). If we include Genesis 2 in our comparison, we also see that references to the Tree of Life bookend the scriptures as they are only found in that chapter and the final chapter of Revelation. All this fits well with the understanding that Revelation was crafted with at least some concern to complement Genesis in function and motifs as well as position in the scriptures.

[11] The same sorts of problems are encountered when trying to synthesise Genesis 1 and 2.

[12] Poythres highlights this theme of counterfeit in Revelation in *The Returning King* (Phillipsburg: P&R Publishing, 2000). In his Tyndale commentary on *Revelation* (Leicester: Intervarsity Press, 1971), Leon Morris suggests that 666 symbolises the repeated falling short of the perfect seven. In looking at the symbolism of Revelation, we again find that it proves a good complement to Genesis.

[13] Even though there is some variation in the pattern of days such that the statement 'And God saw that ... was good' is missing from days two and five, the statement occurs twice on days three and six, ensuring a total of seven occurrences in the chapter.

[14] This was also pointed out to me by Tim Hill.

[15] See note 285 above.

[16] Thinking of the music industry, it's very common for popular songs to use the days of the week device. Any number of bands have walked us through the week as they've told stories through song.

[17] For example, there are strong connections between the New Atheism movement and the gay lobby. This is not because a disproportionally large number of rational thinkers are gay, but because in atheism, gay-friendly groups find a strong ally against the institutionalised religion that has so regularly had a hand in suppressing their freedoms and condemning their actions. This is not just a rational relationship, but one that is highly emotional and political.

[18] It is also appears a few times later in Gn 25:12, 19; 36:1, 9; 37:2.

Chapter 10: Grounds for Divorce?

Science, scientism and the Christian faith[1]

Chris Mulherin

Introduction

'Irreconcilable differences' is the catch-all phrase that, in many legal jurisdictions including Australia, is the sole ground for no-fault divorce. The phrase is deliberately vague, avoiding the need to specify exactly where the differences lie and whether they are irreconcilable. A twelve-month period of separation is deemed to prove irreconcilability.

Like all lasting marriages, faith and the natural sciences have had to work at their relationship over many years. But despite their disagreements, reports of irreconcilable differences are simply untrue. Science and Christian faith are not only compatible but can look forward to a long and happy marriage as they work together in the pursuit of truth.

The so-called 'conflict thesis'—that science and religion are largely incompatible—is an old one that has been thoroughly debunked by both historians and philosophers of science. More recently however, the thesis has been given new life by an alignment of special interests: the financial interests of the publishing industry, the media's penchant for conflict stories, and the anti-theistic preaching of a new breed of would-be public intellectuals such as the figurehead of the so-called New Atheism, Richard Dawkins; people who have little respect for either serious historical or rigorous philosophical inquiry.

It is true that history records many conflicts between people or groups who have been seen as representatives of science and religion. However, historical examples of disagreement do not amount to philosophical or theological incompatibility (just as my wife and I have our differences but are not incompatible and not headed for divorce). So it is important to get the conflict thesis clear to begin with: differences of opinion do not constitute serious conflict—after all, even science itself is rife with differences of opinion. If the conflict thesis is to have any credibility, it cannot be simply about whether representatives of religion or of science have had their differences; a conflict thesis worth pondering is one that suggests that there is a necessary and fundamental conflict between science and faith. In this essay I hope to illuminate some aspects of the nature of both science and faith, and in the process to show that the rumours of irreconcilable differences are based more on misunderstanding than on the real character of the parties concerned.

This chapter is written for the layperson, of whatever faith or none, in an attempt to clarify some key misunderstandings that arise when discussion of science and faith warms up. I am aware that I may frustrate the more philosophically-minded reader as I neglect many nuances of the science-and-religion relationship. Unfortunately, more detailed crossing of philosophical t's and dotting of philosophical i's would only confuse the issue.

As my subtitle suggests I am going to tackle this topic by looking at three key terms: science, scientism and Christian faith. But why Christianity? It is notoriously difficult to define 'religion'; there are many religions, some theistic, some polytheistic and some which do not have a God or gods. So, for the sake of discussion in a Western context, where Christianity is the majority religion and is also the brunt of the most vigorous attacks of the so-called New Atheism, it is the relationship between science and orthodox Christian belief that I will discuss here.

I will suggest ten ideas that are central to a clear understanding of the science-Christianity relationship. Each of these is an attempt to clarify the commonly used words and concepts caught up in common thinking about a so-called conflict between science and religion. Just as in any marriage much depends on clear communication; unless we clarify some aspects of the nature of science, and also clarify what we mean by religion, there is no possibility of clear-headed discussion and it may appear that differences are irreconcilable. So, let's start with religion and then turn to science before finishing with an aberration of science, known as scientism.

Christianity

The first idea worth remembering is this: Christianity is a world-view; it's about meanings and not mechanisms.

Christianity is a world-view: It's about meanings, not mechanisms

One of the dangers of referring to the so-called science-religion relationship is that this very description suggests a symmetry between two comparable entities: science on the one hand, and faith on the other. But science and Christian faith are not directly comparable, because Christianity is a world-view while science is not and never can be.

A world-view is a set of ideas and beliefs that offers a coherent framework with which to interpret the universe and the human condition. It's a sketch of the 'big picture'. It answers such questions as: 'How should we live?' 'What happens after death?' 'Does life have a meaning?' 'Does God exist?' 'What does it mean to be human?' We could say that it answers questions about meaning. Although a world-view may not answer every question, it still tells us where the answers lie and it aims to be coherent in the answers it does give. This means that it cannot contain glaring contradictions within its set of core beliefs.

What sort of beliefs does the Christian world-view consist of? Christian orthodox belief includes a 'supernatural' creator God who made the universe and everything in it. Christianity includes the possibility of miracles, the death and bodily resurrection of Jesus Christ and the linear nature of history from creation through to final consummation. It also includes an understanding of the purposes of humanity, which is shaped in the image of God and made for relationship with God. And Christianity holds that humanity is incapable of knowing and loving God perfectly, so humans are dependent on God for both revelation and for restoring the relationship with their creator.

This description of the Christian world-view implies that it is answering questions about meaning and not mechanics; about the purposes, and not the particles, of the universe. But it doesn't answer all possible questions and it would be a mistake to think that it should, just as it would be a mistake to think that science has answers to every type of question. The implications of this are clear: Christianity is not directly comparable to science because science is not a world-view and Christianity is not science.

Christianity is not science

For the sake of discussion, let's think of science in terms of physics or biology or chemistry or astronomy. These are natural sciences which search for the mechanisms and laws of the universe in the hope of answering the 'how' questions; they look for the physical causes and constituents of what goes on in our world.

Christianity is different: on the one hand, as a world-view Christianity is much more encompassing than science because it answers the big questions such as: 'Why are we here?' or 'Why is there something rather than nothing?' Conversely, Christianity has little interest in other sorts of issues, some of which we might call the 'how' questions. Think for example of the vexed question of the New Testament model for a perfect church. At my church, we wrestle with how best to structure a multi-congregation and multi-site church. We would love a blueprint, but while the Bible tells us the meaning of the Church and offers some general principles, it contains no description of the mechanics of setting up the perfect church. In the area of moral guidance too, the Bible offers a general foundation for our thinking and acting, but it does not tell us exactly how to run a country or how to order our finances.

So Christianity is not science and it is a mistake to think that the Bible is a political treatise or a scientific textbook. In fact when it comes to biblical interpretation, the Christian tradition has always recognised that there are various ways of reading scripture and that the Bible is made up of a number of different types of literature. In short, to quote Galileo Galilei, 'The Bible teaches how to go to heaven not how the heavens go'.[2]

It's time now to turn to the second area of discussion, that of science.

Science

Science is not a world-view: It's about mechanisms, not meanings

Science for its part is not a world-view. Physics and chemistry do not make claims about the meaning or purposes of particles or molecules. Biology and astronomy do not tell us the meaning of spiny anteaters or spiral galaxies. That's simply not what they're about, and if we look to science to answer such questions we ask more than it can offer.

As for the difference between a world-view (which answers questions of meaning and purpose) and the pursuit of science (which answers questions about mechanisms and natural causes), perhaps an illustrative cup of tea will help clarify matters. If I ask, as I put the kettle on the stove to boil, 'Why is the water boiling?', how might we answer the question? That depends on how we understood the 'why' in the question: is the 'why' asking about meaning or mechanism? The alert physics student, focusing on the mechanics of the situation, might answer that the water is boiling due to the raised energy levels of the molecules of water induced by the heat from the stove. To which I might reply by putting a tea bag in a cup and suggesting that actually the water is boiling because I want a cup of tea. Both answers are correct, but what they show is that the question, 'Why is the water boiling?' is ambiguous. In fact it is two questions in one. It could be a question about mechanics—'What causes the water to boil?'—or it could be a question about meaning—'What is the purpose of the water boiling?'

There are many such questions that can be understood in two ways and it is helpful to clarify how we interpret them before we try to answer them. 'Why are we here?' has both a theological and a scientific answer, and 'Why is she crying?' has an answer in terms of brain chemistry and neuronal firings that is hardly a sufficient answer in a pastoral setting.

So, we have clarified at least two sorts of questions and answers, which, as shorthand, I am referring to as those about meanings and those about mechanisms. And if, as I have suggested, science is about mechanisms and not meanings then we can see that there are limits to science imposed by the nature of the sorts of questions we ask of it and the sorts of answers we expect.

These limitations of science can be seen in at least two different sorts of difficulties it faces. First are the sort of questions that we might imagine science answering one day, and second are the impossible issues which science will never explain because they lie outside its domain. Let's turn first to some of the difficult questions in science that may one day be resolved. After that we will look at the sorts of questions that science by its nature will never be able to answer.

Science has practical limits: It can't know everything

While science has been enormously successful in revealing the truth of the world around us there are some questions that make us realise that we are very far from knowing everything about the natural world and there may even be practical limits to our knowledge. Of course the limits of current science are not an argument for some form of theism—that would be to fall into a 'God of the gaps' argument—but they do serve to make us wary about making overly bold claims about scientific knowledge. I'm thinking of challenges to science such as the following:

- *How the universe began*: Stephen Hawking, the world's most famous cosmologist, postulates the spontaneous creation of the universe. He says, 'The universe began with the Big Bang, which simply followed the inevitable law of physics. Because there is a law such as gravity, the universe can and will create itself from nothing … The universe didn't need a God to begin; it was quite capable of launching its existence on its own'.[3] Now this sort of statement is wonderful for newspaper headlines but is a particularly clear case of passing the explanatory buck from one level of explanation to another. Even if his theory is right, Hawking hasn't explained how the universe comes into existence out of nothing; he has proposed that it comes into existence out of the laws of physics, which existed prior to the universe as we know it. While atheists frown on Christians for using God as an explanation, Hawking uses the laws of physics, and gravity in particular, as if they themselves demand no explanation.

• *Gravity*: speaking of gravity, a popular history of science subject at The University of Melbourne ended last year with the following memorable words: 'After 2500 years of searching for the answer, natural philosophers and scientists still don't know why things fall down'.[4]

• *Dark matter*: according to current theories, most of the universe (about 83%) seems to be made up of 'dark matter' which cannot be seen because it does not reflect or emit light. We have no idea what type of matter it is but its existence is postulated in order to explain observations about the known stars and galaxies.

• *Fine tuning*: the laws of the universe appear to be fine-tuned for the existence of life. There are various fundamental constants of the universe that if they were slightly different would render it impossible for life to have developed at all. Is it coincidence that we live in such a universe? The main proposed explanation extends the bounds of believability. It's called the multiverse theory and postulates myriad parallel universes covering all the possible values of the fundamental constants. Physicist Paul Davies says this about the multiverse theory: 'Invoking an infinity of unseen universes to explain the unusual features of the one we do see is just as ad hoc as invoking an unseen Creator. The multiverse theory may be dressed up in scientific language, but in essence it requires the same leap of faith'.[5]

• *The origins of life* or abiogenesis (not to mention the definition of 'life', but that's another story): while evolutionary theory assumes that all life is descended from an original life form, we seem as far as ever from seriously explaining the spontaneous generation of the first replicating life from non-life. And, in the words of Francis Collins, the ex-head of the Human Genome Project and now

Director of the US National Institutes of Health, 'Now, if you were able in a laboratory situation to create something that was capable of self-replication, that wouldn't prove that's how it happened; it probably would be way off from whatever happened'.[6]

- *Consciousness*: the struggle to understand the subjective aspects of consciousness has recently extended from philosophy to neuroscience. But while correlations have been revealed between brain states and the feelings and attitudes that we attribute to consciousness, we are no closer to understanding how any particular brain state can be mapped on to 'what it is like to be me'. As one respected physicist puts it, 'it is the only major question in the sciences that we don't even know how to ask'.[7]

- *Free will*: while we all act as if we have free will, a strictly naturalistic view of human beings seems to lead to the conclusion that everything that we do or say or think is ultimately determined by strict causal laws or by random sub-atomic events. Normal life including science itself assumes and depends on human freedom of choice, yet explaining how a strictly biological view of human beings is compatible with that freedom is scientifically and philosophically out of our reach at present.

These are some of the difficult questions that science faces. However, that does not mean they are insurmountable; it is conceivable that one day science will have answers to most of them. But let's turn now from the difficult to the impossible questions; those issues that science can't explain because they lie outside science altogether. We will particularly focus on some unprovable assumptions that underlie the scientific enterprise. These are not like the practical limits to science which seem very difficult to overcome because they are philosophical or logical limits; they are limitations imposed on science by the very nature of science itself.

Science has philosophical limits: It relies on presuppositions

As a pursuit of knowledge about the natural world, the natural sciences cannot delve into philosophical, logical or religious questions. The sciences cannot do so because such questions are not the subject matter of science. But that does not mean that science can leave such issues aside.

The life and breath of science lies in its rigorous approach to uncovering the truth of the natural world based on certain working assumptions, which it does not question. This recognition that science doesn't start from a blank slate, that science must assume some things to even get off the ground, is captured by atheist philosopher Daniel Dennett, who warns of the risk of a naïve attitude to science that fails to see its philosophical foundations: 'There is no such thing as philosophy-free science; there is only science whose philosophical baggage is taken on board without examination'.[8] So, as C. S. Lewis explains in his excellent little book *Miracles*, the philosophical question must come first.[9]

One way of thinking about these philosophical assumptions is that they are like tools of the trade, which we use to produce results. In order to drive a nail, the carpenter uses a hammer without questioning it. The focus is on the nail; the hammer is taken for granted. So too science takes for granted its foundational assumptions, but it cannot justify them scientifically; they must come first, before science begins its work.

So what are some of these foundational philosophical assumptions of science?

- Science can only be practised by assuming that **the universe is governed by laws**; that there are laws of nature which result in the possibility of repeatable experiments. This means that in the laboratory, the scientist must assume that the results of an experiment are due to the laws of nature and not to either random or supernatural causes. This assumption governs the scientist's methods of going about science and it is an assumption that cannot be proven.

- This regularity or uniformity that science is based on is revealed in the way that **science depends on induction**. Inductive argument is the process of observing repeated events or experience or experimental results and drawing the conclusion that future or unobservable events will follow the same pattern. For example, if I observe a million swans and they are all white I might conclude that all swans are white. But as this case shows, induction is not foolproof; Charles Darwin arrived in Australia and found black swans. Science simply has no way of justifying its confidence in induction. And if you are tempted to say that induction is obviously valid because it has worked in the past, think again: that would involve an inductive justification of induction, which is the very thing we are seeking to justify. This conundrum is what philosophers call 'the problem of induction' and the logical fallacy involved is known as 'begging the question'.

• Science must assume, as we all do, that **there is a world 'out there'** independent of whatever human beings might think or say about it. And science must also assume that the world is knowable. It is notoriously difficult to rigorously prove the existence of the 'external world'. It is something we simply accept as true without question and it seems absurd to demand proofs for what we take to be so obviously true.

• Science must also assume that **human reasoning leads to truth.** Why do we believe that our reasoning and memory and sensory functions are sound and lead to truth? Again, we cannot prove these presuppositions because they are assumptions we must make in order to even think about any sort of proofs or argument. The possibility of truth and the validity of basic rules of logic are also assumptions we must make before we can begin a rational conversation. You can't argue for the reliability of logic without using logic. So, for example, we must take for granted that you cannot assert one thing and its contradiction without falling into incoherence. Either all swans are white or they are not, but you can't have it both ways, and if you think you can then you leave yourself out of rational conversation.

• Meanwhile, talking of rational conversation, another 'pre-scientific' assumption that we rely on—even as your eyes scan the black marks on this page—is that our **language is adequate to describe the external world** and to converse with others about it.

Such are some of the foundational but unprovable beliefs of science. Now we turn to one more limit of science and it's the one that presents the most problems in the science and religion discussion. It's the crucial issue of the relationship of science to naturalism.

Philosophical naturalism is a world-view

Philosophical naturalism (usually just called naturalism) is the view that there is no God or gods and that the natural world that science investigates is all that there is. According to philosophical naturalism, reality is only made up of 'natural' components such as matter and energy. Negatively, philosophical naturalism claims that the supernatural does not exist. In its cruder forms it equates Christianity and other faiths to belief in fairies at the bottom of the garden, celestial teapots, and the Flying Spaghetti Monster. Or in the words of philosopher Friedrich Nietzsche, Christians believe in things that don't exist.[10]

Expressed this way we can see that philosophical naturalism is a world-view in competition with other world-views. It is a belief system that answers (mostly negatively) the questions of meaning we mentioned above. Now let's complicate matters by introducing another sort of naturalism: *methodological* naturalism. At the heart of a good understanding of the relationship between science and faith is the difference between *philosophical* naturalism and *methodological* naturalism, which is not a world-view and is an essential foundation of science.

Science is based on methodological naturalism

Methodological naturalism is simply the assumption that when we do science there is no supernatural intervention taking place. The role of science is quite appropriately to look for natural explanations, so supernatural causes are ruled out in the laboratory and in scientific thinking. Like the carpenter's hammer, methodological naturalism is a tool used in order to get on with the job. So although the scientist who uses the tool of methodological naturalism may be a religious believer, their religious belief plays no part in the way they do their experiments.

The success of science does not prove that philosophical naturalism is true

Now we arrive at a major source of confusion. Much of the claimed conflict between science and faith arises from confusing the tool of *methodological* naturalism with a commitment to the world-view of *philosophical* naturalism (or simply naturalism). This is particularly evident when people ask a question such as, 'But doesn't science disprove religion?' It seems that what lies behind such thinking is an argument that goes something like this:

- Science is based on naturalism.
- Science is successful.
- So naturalism must be true.
- Naturalism and Christianity are mutually exclusive world-views.
- So, Christianity must be false.

Now, there is a major flaw in this argument. There is sleight of hand where the word 'naturalism' is used in two different ways. We can see this if we rewrite the first part of the argument more clearly as follows:

- Science is based on *methodological* naturalism ('God does not intervene in our experiments'.)
- Science is successful.
- *Philosophical* naturalism ('there is no God') must be true.

But as we can see, the conclusion doesn't follow because the conclusion talks about *philosophical* naturalism while the first line talks about *methodological* naturalism which is another thing altogether. In simple terms and without the formalities,

In simple terms, and without the formalities, just because science assumes that God does not intervene in scientific experiments (*methodological* naturalism) it does not follow that God does not exist (*philosophical* naturalism). So the success of science can only lead us to conclude, at most, that if God exists then God normally allows the laws of nature to take their course. Science seeks truth about the natural world by using the tool of methodological naturalism but it is not committed to philosophical naturalism which is a world-view.

Before turning to *scientism*, which reveals the logic of philosophical naturalism taken to its extreme, we will first look a little more at an aspect of science that is often forgotten. That is, the intrinsically human element in science.

Science is a human enterprise relying on human judgment and integrity

We have seen that science has philosophical limits and that it must take many things for granted without proving them. One corollary of this is that there are no foolproof means of arriving at scientific conclusions. In the words of atheist physicist Richard Feynman, 'scientific knowledge is a body of statements of varying degrees of certainty—some most unsure, some nearly sure, but none absolutely certain'.[11]

Science never 'proves' a theory (except perhaps in mathematics). It is true that some theories become so taken for granted that they become 'laws', but strictly speaking, they have not been proven so much as rigorously tested and supported by the evidence. The human causes of climate change for example will never be proven or found with absolute certainty to be true. So the skeptics have a point: we cannot prove that anthropogenic climate change is occurring. This is because, in the words of scientist and philosopher Michael Polanyi, scientific findings 'could conceivably be false'.[12] Or, as Simon Conway Morris says when comparing faith and science, 'both depend on passionate beliefs, where questioning of received dogma can swiftly lead to raised voices and dangerously flushed faces.[13]

If we can never prove the truth of a scientific theory, some philosophers of science have suggested that at least we might be able to know conclusively that a theory is false. This view of science (called 'falsificationism') says that theories can be falsified by the results of an experiment. In fact what happens more often than not is that, rather than questioning a theory, we assume there is a problem with the experiment or the observations. Do you remember your high school science experiments, which invariably produced aberrant results? If observations contradicted the theory, did you assume you had falsified a long-held truth of science? More likely you did what is standard practice in science: you made a judgment call about where the problem lay, recognising that there could be any number of reasons why your experimental results didn't match the theory.

So, despite widespread misunderstanding, there is not a rigid scientific method that guarantees truth. Instead scientists rely on rules of thumb or maxims such as 'Ockham's razor' which says that a simpler theory should be preferred over a complex one if both have the same explanatory power. So in the end, every conclusion of science and every interpretation of experimental results is just that: an interpretation. It is one interpretation—in a sense, subjective—made by a real flesh-and-blood human being about what their senses are telling them and about its significance. And the history of science is full of cases where different scientists have interpreted the same data differently—think of Copernicus who reinterpreted the astronomical data and suggested that the sun and not the earth was at the centre of the solar system.

This dependence of science on human factors is also shown up in its corporate nature. Think back again to the school laboratory. One reason that you were happy to abandon your high school experimental results was because you trusted the integrity of those who had gone before you: your teacher, the authors of the textbook, the peer reviewers of scientific papers and the authors of those papers, some living, some centuries dead. Isaac Newton, perhaps the world's most famous scientist, was under no illusion about his own dependence on those who had gone before him. In a letter to his rival Robert Hooke, he says, 'If I have seen further it is by standing on the shoulders of giants'.[14] Every scientist is similarly dependent on the results, judgments and theories of others that together make up the web of science.

To sum up, the practice of science is an intrinsically human pursuit, full of the subjective judgments that that implies, and it is dependent on a web of trust between scientists who are assumed to share personal moral commitments to truth and integrity. But this picture of science I have described is disconcerting to many and especially to those who see in science the one and only means of access to truth.

Scientism

Scientism is an aberration of science

So far, we have teased out a little of the nature of science and we have highlighted the importance of clarifying what we mean when we speak of religion. We have also seen that there are many differences between science and faith, the most obvious being that they focus on different objects of enquiry and that they attempt to answer different sorts of questions. We have seen that by clarifying those sorts of questions, as well as the nature of the underlying assumptions of science, the threat of an inevitable and fundamental conflict diminishes.

Let's turn now to an extreme version of naturalism, often referred to as scientism. In the discussion of naturalism we saw the danger of making overly bold claims for science. We also saw that there are many presuppositions of science that underlie scientific practice but which cannot be arrived at by using science; that is, science cannot show that its own presuppositions are valid. But scientism rides roughshod over these subtleties.

Scientism is a word which is usually used in a derogatory manner to describe a naive, almost blind, faith in science. It is the idea that only scientific knowledge is authentic and any other sort of knowledge is meaningless nonsense. The thinking behind scientism goes like this: if a naturalistic world-view is correct—that is, if there is no God or gods and the natural world is all that there is—then the only possible knowledge we can have of anything is scientific knowledge. So all that 'is' and all that 'can be known' is verifiable or falsifiable through the scientific method, and whatever can't in principle be analysed and measured by science is empty belief and fantasy. So, where naturalism is a belief about what sorts of things exist in the world, scientism takes this one step further and says that the only things we can know, and know about, are revealed by science. The corollary is that anything that cannot (in principle) be known by 'the scientific method' cannot even be discussed sensibly.

Thus science is held up as the absolute authority in every area of human life and thinking. Instead of science being a tool in the search for truth it has become an ideology—some would say a quasi-religion—that constrains what sort of truths are allowed to exist. Philosopher Daniel Dennett, one of the prominent so-called New Atheists, captures this view when he says, 'When it comes to facts, and explanations of facts, science is the only game in town'.[15]

So what is the problem with scientism? To put it bluntly, scientism is a faith and blind faith at that. It is one thing to humbly and cautiously adopt naturalism as a world-view—one can believe that the natural is all that there is without being dogmatic—but it is another thing to make bold claims about science being 'the only game in town' or to suggest that science can show that naturalism is correct.

At the heart of scientism lies a logical contradiction. Scientism claims to be rigorously scientific and says that we should believe something along the following lines: 'The only things you should believe are those things that science shows us to be true'. Let's call that the 'S-thesis'. Now reread the S-thesis again. A moment's thought reveals the contradiction at the core of scientism. If we are to believe the S-thesis (that is, that we should believe only scientific claims) then why should we believe the S-thesis, which is not a scientific claim? In fact taking the S-thesis seriously means that we should disbelieve the S-thesis itself. In this way scientism seems to be an attempt to lift itself up by the bootstraps, or, to change the metaphor, the S-thesis shoots itself in the foot.

There are many things we believe that are not the result of science. And as we have already seen, there are many presuppositions that science depends on but which science cannot show to be true. If science were the only game in town then it would put itself out of business because the game of science depends on so many 'non-scientific' beliefs. But as most scientists, religious or otherwise, know well, science is not scientism and scientism does not follow from science: it is one thing to affirm the validity of scientific knowledge but it is another thing to say that all knowledge must be scientific.[16]

Conclusion: Conflict? What conflict?

For most Christians with a healthy respect for natural science it comes as no surprise that science and faith are not locked in mortal combat. For the Christian, all truth is God's truth and, to use Francis Bacon's metaphor, both the book of God's word and the book of his works reveal something of the creator of all things. Science and Christianity are neither in conflict nor are they completely independent. They are, as Simon Conway Morris points out, more like conjoined twins and if they are seen as mutually incompatible the consequences are dire:

> Science without Christianity is actually rudderless, doomed to investigate a universe in ever greater detail, but in a way that Nietzsche would have appreciated, as a completely meaningless exercise. And Christianity? Without science it risks sinking back into pantheism, abandoning rationality for a gobbledegook of syncretistic tosh.[17]

To those convinced that a divorce is imminent, let me suggest that the marriage will endure. Truly 'the church of God is an anvil that has worn out many hammers' and while the New Testament exhorts Christians to 'be prepared to give an answer' to those who ask the reason for their hope,[18] there is, from a Christian perspective, no cause for alarm. The universe is in good hands and they are not those of Stephen Hawking or Richard Dawkins.

---

[1] This chapter is based on Chris Mulherin, "The Marriage of Heaven and Hell? Faith, the Natural Sciences and Rumours of Divorce," in *God and Science in*

Classroom and Pulpit, ed. Graham Buxton, Chris Mulherin, and Mark Worthing (Preston, Victoria: Mosaic Press, 2012).

[2] Galileo is the central figure in the most famous so-called conflict between science and religion. Some of his thoughts on the Bible and science are worth quoting:

> 'The reason produced for condemning the opinion that the earth moves and the sun stands still is that in many places in the Bible one may read that the sun moves and the earth stands still. Since the Bible cannot err, it follows as a necessary consequence that anyone takes an erroneous and heretical position who maintains that the sun is inherently motionless and the earth movable. With regard to this argument, I think in the first place that it is very pious to say and prudent to affirm that the Holy Bible can never speak untruth—whenever its true meaning is understood. But I believe that nobody will deny that it is often very abstruse, and may say things which are quite different from what its bare words signify. Hence in expounding the Bible if one were always to confine oneself to the unadorned grammatical meaning, one might fall into error. ... Thus it would be necessary to assign to God feet, hands and eyes'. Galileo Galilei, *Discoveries and Opinions of Galileo*, trans., Stillman Drake (Garden City: Doubleday, 1957), 181.

[3] Stephen Hawking and Leonard Mlodinow, *The Grand Design* (New York: Bantam Books, 2010).

[4] HPSC10001 'From Plato to Einstein' is taught by Dr Kristian Camilleri.

[5] Paul Davies, 'A Brief history of the Multiverse', *New York Times*, April 12, 2003. At http://www.nytimes.com/2003/04/12/opinion/a-brief-history-of-the-multiverse.html. Last accessed 15 February, 2012.

[6] Interview, May 10, 2005 (accessed 29 February, 2012). At http://www.pbs.org/wgbh/nova/tech/collins-genome.html.

[7] James Trefil, *One Hundred and One Things You Don't Know About Science and No One Else Does Either* (New York: Mariner Books, 1997), 15.

[8] Daniel Dennett, *Darwin's Dangerous Idea: Evolution and the Meanings of Life* (London: Penguin Books 1995), 21.

[9] C. S. Lewis, *Miracles* (Glasgow: Collins, 1977), 8.

[10] Friedrich Wilhelm Nietzsche, Aaron Ridley and Judith Norman, *The Anti-Christ, Ecce Homo, Twilight of the Idols, and Other Writings*, Cambridge Texts in the History of Philosophy (New York: Cambridge University Press, 2005), 183.

[11] Richard P. Feynman and Jeffrey Robbins, *The Pleasure of Finding Things Out: The Best Short Works of Richard P. Feynman* (Cambridge, Mass.: Perseus Books, 1999), 146.

[12] Michael Polanyi, *Personal Knowledge* (London: Routledge & Kegan Paul, 1958), 214.

[13] Simon Conway Morris. 'Skin-deep differences? The Mystical Marriage of Science and Religion'. Address given at Magdalen College Chapel, Oxford, February 12, 2012. (Accessed 29 February, 2012)
At: www.magd.ox.ac.uk/__data/assets/pdf_file/0019/15760/12-Feb-12-SCM.pdf.

[14] Isaac Newton, *The Correspondence of Isaac Newton, Volume 1*, ed. H. W. Turnbull (New York: Cambridge University Press, 1961), 416.

[15] Daniel Dennett, interview in *New Statesman*, April 10, 2006 (accessed 29 February, 2012). http://www.newstatesman.com/200604100019.

[16] Alex Rosenberg is one of the few philosophers or scientists happy to accept the label of scientism. In his book *The Atheist's Guide to Reality: Enjoying Life Without Illusions* (New York: W. W. Norton, 2011) Rosenberg challenges the cowardice of scientists who cover up the truth rather than admit that science (and in particular physics) offers all the answers that there are. For a summary version see the article by Rosenberg at http://onthehuman.org/2009/11/the-disenchanted-naturalists-guide-to-reality/. (accessed February 29, 2012).

[17] Conway Morris.

[18] 1 Pr 3:15.

About the Authors

Dr Simon Angus

Dr Simon Angus is a Senior Lecturer in the Dept. of Economics at Monash University. With an eclectic background in Science, Engineering, Arts and Economics, he teaches and researches in the Science of Complexity and Agent-based Modelling. He is married to Susan and has two children: a daughter, Hannah May (2.5 yrs), and a newborn to meet in May 2012.

Simon's spiritual journey started in a 'God-fearing' household, and an Anglican school, before seeing him embrace literary criticism and existentialist philosophy as an undergrad which took him to nihilism as a 'holding-pattern' whilst he gave meaning the benefit of the doubt. Eventually, confronted with the Gospels of Jesus, and close Christian friends whose lives were confoundingly different, he got round to investigating the historicity of Jesus. Surprisingly, he found himself accepting the gospel's version of events as the most reasonable explanation for the events surrounding Jesus' death. That was in Summer 2000/2001.

Since then, seeing many of his colleagues taken up with scientism, he's been interested to present a 'reasonable faith' at any occasion, engaging in dialogue and through writing with atheist claims.

Rev'd Phillip Brown

Phillip Brown is the Priest In Charge at St John's Brunswick West in Melbourne and has a keen interest in the New Atheism. Phillip petitioned the Melbourne Synod to establish the Christianity and Atheism Committee and as a member wrote their apologetic brochure 'Christians Answering Atheists'. Phillip holds an Associate in Music Performance (Piano) and a Bachelor of Arts (Honours) in Philosophy as well as a Master in Divinity. Phillip's wife Lisa lectures in youth ministry at Ridley Melbourne and they both enjoy Christian ministry and their dog Moses.

Dr Justin Denholm

Justin Denholm is a physician and ethicist, and has co-ordinated the Centre for Applied Christian Ethics at Ridley Melbourne Mission and Ministry College since 2008. His recent book *Talking About Ethics* (Acorn Press, 2011) is a practical introduction in developing skills for better conversations about ethical issues, which he hopes will get a good workout during the Global Atheist Convention!

Justin and his family attend St John's Anglican Church in Brunswick West, Victoria, where they enjoy many challenging conversations about ethics and faith.

Mr Robert Martin

Robert Martin heads up the City Bible Forum in Melbourne, a national mission to city workers. His ongoing interest in atheism is sparked by a desire to understand and know the truth, 'If Christ has not been raised, our preaching is useless and so is your faith' (1 Corinthians 15:14). Whilst studying at theological college Robert decided that if he were pursuing vocational theological ministry he'd want assurance that his faith wasn't merely a delusion. Hence Robert engaged the works of Richard Dawkins. This led to a challenging and stimulating period of thinking and growth and culminated in Robert writing his honours thesis at theological college on the works of the New Atheists. Ultimately Robert found the claims of the New Atheists unconvincing and deeply flawed. Robert attends St Jude's Anglican Church in Parkville is married to Di and they have three young children, Aiden, Aoife and Callum.

Rev'd Chris Mulherin

Chris Mulherin is an Anglican minister currently researching a doctorate in philosophy of science and theology. He is also interim minister of the Unichurch congregations at St Jude's Anglican church in Parkville. Chris lived for 13 years in Argentina with his wife Lindy and their five boys where they worked with university students and the Anglican Church. He has taught engineering, philosophy and theology.

Rev'd Tim Patrick

Tim Patrick is a Melbourne-based Anglican minister who holds a Master of Divinity and a Bachelor of Science with a first class honours in geology. He is currently working towards a doctorate in history. Tim attends St John's Church in Brunswick West with his family.

Dr Gordon Preece

Dr Gordon Preece was a youth worker, an assistant minister and rector at several Anglican churches in Sydney and is now the part-time senior minister at Yarraville Anglican in Melbourne. Academically, he lectured at Morling Baptist College Sydney and was Director of the Centre for Applied Christian Ethics at Ridley Melbourne and Director of Macquarie Christian Studies Institute. Most recently Gordon was Executive Director of Urban Seed, a ministry of hospitality and advocacy for homeless people in Melbourne. He is currently an ethics consultant for Christian Super and teaches ethics for Ridley Melbourne and business ethics for the School of Applied Finance at Macquarie University as well as being part-time; Director of Ethos: EA Centre for Christianity and Society. Gordon's passion for connecting scripture and culture apologetically aroused his interest in the current New Atheist challenge. He is author/editor of eleven books and of *Zadok Perspectives*, with three more books forthcoming in 2012.

Dr Greg Restall

Greg Restall is Associate Professor of Philosophy at The University of Melbourne. He received his PhD from The University of Queensland in 1994. His research focuses on logic, metaphysics, the philosophy of language, and even some philosophy of religion. He has published over 70 papers in journals and collections, and is the author of three books, *An Introduction to Substructural Logics* (Routledge, 2000), *Logic* (Routledge, 2006), and *Logical Pluralism* (Oxford University Press, 2006; with JC

Beall). He first got into philosophy because he wanted to reflect on his Christian faith, and he found the tools and techniques of philosophy not only useful, but a great deal of fun, too. He likes reflecting on atheism because lots of his friends are atheists and he wants to understand points of agreement and disagreement, He attends St John's Anglican Church in Brunswick West.